Cubs Fans'
LEADERSHIP
SECRETS

"This book helps you
create high-standard leadership
success at every turn."

———

"Do you want to become
a more powerful leader and
inspire people to do
their best? Read this book."

———

Cubs Fans'
LEADERSHIP
SECRETS

John Charles Kunich
and
Richard I. Lester

Parkhurst Brothers Inc., Publishers

Little Rock, Arkansas

www.pbros.net

Parkhurst Brothers books are distributed to the trade through the University of Chicago Press Distribution Center. Copies of this and other Parkhurst Brothers Inc., Publishers titles are available to organizations and corporations for purchase in quantity by contacting Special Sales Department at our home office location, listed on our web site.

Printed in the United States of America

First Edition, 2009

12 11 10 9 8 7 6 5 4 3 2 1

Library of Congress LCCN :   2008909925

ISBN: 978-1-935166-02-3 [10 digit: 1-935166-02-6]

This book is printed on archival-quality paper that meets requirements of the American National Standard for Information Sciences, Permanence of Paper, Printed Library Materials, ANSI Z39.48-1984.

Book design and cover design:
WENDELL E. HALL

Page composition:
SHELLY CULBERTSON

Acquired for Parkhurst Brothers Inc., Publishers by:
TED PARKHURST

Editor:
ROGER ARMBRUST

Proofreaders:
BARBARA AND BILL PADDACK

Acknowledgements

I thank my wife, Marcia K. Vigil-Kunich, for her support through my long addiction to the Cubs. I also thank our two daughters, Christina Laurel "Christie" Kunich and JulieKate Marva Kunich who, although they were born in China and have never lived in Chicago, have learned to understand and comfort their dad when he bleeds Cubbie blue. I thank my unequalled research assistant, Rose G. Proto, for her splendid and amazingly insightful work, made even more remarkable by the fact that she's been a Yankees fan from birth. Finally, I am truly grateful to the wondrous Cubs heroes who have given me so much to cheer for my entire life, during the longest championship drought in baseball history. Standing at the head of this long, glorious list are Ernie Banks, Billy Williams, Ferguson Jenkins, Ron Santo, and Ryne Sandberg.

—JOHN CHARLES KUNICH

Dedications

To Chicago Cubs fans and players everywhere who have lived and loved their entire lives yearning for just one World Series championship; and to everyone like them who dares to dream an impossible dream.

—JOHN CHARLES KUNICH

To the men and women of Air University, the intellectual and leadership center of the Air Force, who strive to develop America's Airmen today... for tomorrow, and to achieve Integrity, Service, and Excellence. And to Cub fans everywhere.

—RICHARD I. LESTER

Table of Contents

Individual Success Does Not Guarantee Team Victory
Cubs teams have often focused on one or two star performers, a detriment to
the team's overall performance. Stars have often been selfish and devoted to their
own success, and the leaders have tolerated this. Effective leadership recognizes
this dangerous situation and provides an antidote.

Don't Count Your Pennants Before They're Won
The Cubs have lost championships by failing to pay attention to the matters at
hand, and taking for granted their current successful position. As a result, they
have suffered notable late-season collapses. Leaders must balance proactive
planning with effective engagement in immediate tasks the team faces.

Farm for the Future
A major reason for the Cubs' century-long drought: Failure to devote adequate
resources to identifying, attracting, training, and retaining top-quality young
talent. They have foolishly failed to plant and nurture the seeds of their own
success. The leader must obey the harvest law, and recognize the importance
of tending to the team's next generation.

Panic Proves a Poor Strategic Tool
Teams that fail to prepare for emergencies most often fall vulnerable to panic,
resulting in disaster when crises do materialize. Cubs teams have "choked" in the
clutch due to neglecting the groundwork necessary to immunize themselves to
pressure. A good leader understands the factors that comprise a team's Coefficient
of Panic Vulnerability, and takes steps to influence it positively.

Don't Brock Yourself
The Cubs traded away young, future Hall-of-Famer Lou Brock in a misguided and
shortsighted episode of leadership ineptitude. Often, teams do not recognize the
diamonds in the rough when they are right among them. Effective leaders develop
programs to identify and nurture future top performers, and to hold on to them.

Foreword

By Kenneth Blanchard, Ph.D.

You are reading a leadership book that offers something truly new. The vision of *Cubs Fans' Leadership Secrets* is that every leader can benefit from studying the hard lessons learned by the Chicago Cubs baseball team and their millions of devoted fans during a century of losing.

At first, the notion seems to make no sense. How can 100 years of effort, involving well over 100 games each year, teach us anything positive about leadership when the net result of all that struggle is a grand total of precisely zero World Series championships? The Cubs have played more than 15,000 regular-season baseball games since their last World Series triumph in 1908, with not one big prize to show for it. Now, we all believe that everyone deserves a second chance now and then, but 15,000 of them might appear a bit too much.

But think about it. In your own life, haven't you learned at least as much, if not more, from your biggest mistakes than you have from your successes? When we lose, it hurts. And that pain is all too often what it takes to get a difficult lesson into our stubborn and change-resistant brains. Paradoxically, we can gain more from losing than from winning, because losing is such an intense and unpleasant experience that we long remember it and want very much to avoid a repeat performance. The saying "no pain, no gain" reflects this principle that the most important lessons are usually learned only after we pay a high price in the currency of our own suffering.

The good news is that the Cubs and their fans already have done the suffering for you. As John Kunich and Richard Lester ask in this book, why not try to get some payoff from all that sorrow? A century of sensational collapses, missed opportunities, shocking errors, self-inflicted wounds, managerial madness, and dysfunctional internal dynamics makes for an unprecedented longitudinal case study of how *not* to win. Kunich and Lester turn this colossal failure-fest inside out and show exactly what went so wrong for so long, and how today's leaders can learn from these mistakes.

The Cubs have given us an amazingly rich treasure trove of leadership insights, and this book is the first to recognize that fact. We can now harness the ideas born of a hundred years of broken dreams and unbroken failure. By focusing on the converse of all the curses that have plagued the Cubs, Kunich and Lester have uncovered great practical tools we can use to avoid duplicating those defects in our own lives and in our own careers. We can anticipate trouble-spots and steer instead toward hidden areas of potential progress.

Each of the nine chapters, or in baseball terminology, "innings" in this book isolates one of the reasons the Cubs have fallen short for so many decades. These are usually the type of reasonable mistakes we all make—errors that seemed at the time to be right, and misguided but understandable responses to demanding real-world situations. Until and unless we grasp why these miscues were pop flies disguised as home runs, we are on course to repeat them endlessly, in a never-ending variety of new contexts. But diagnosing and acknowledging the problem is only the first step. Every inning then goes on to analyze how one particular type of pitfall can be proactively averted and even turned into a plus factor, in fields very different from the infield and outfield. The principles may have been derived from the baseball diamond, but they are now diamonds that can sparkle in any setting.

The authors conclude each inning with one of the best features from their previous excellent book on leadership, *Survival Kit for Leaders*. They propose several provocative and engaging questions for the readers to work through on their own. The questions are ideal for use in a small group, but can also be profitable even for a solitary reader who is willing to invest the effort needed to think hard about what he or she has just read. This interactive process is instrumental in making *Cubs Fans' Leadership Secrets* a book that is not only informational, but transformational. By reflecting on the questions, we can vicariously experience the lessons for ourselves, and gain ownership of the insights that flow from them.

WARNING: This will sometimes entail recollection of hard choices and painful situations from your life, but it is well worth it. It makes the book your own, and spares you the travail of even worse outcomes that might otherwise be waiting to happen to you.

Cubs fans are deservedly famous for their undying hope that one day their team will again become World Series Champions. Use this book to hitch onto some of that hope for yourself and the teams you lead. Its secrets will help you bring your hopes into the world of tangible reality.

Cubs Fans' Leadership Secrets

By John Charles Kunich and Richard I. Lester[1]

Introduction

Death is easy; being a Cubs fan is hard.

There is no shortage of books and articles explaining the leadership secrets of famously successful leaders. And why not? It makes sense that the preeminent exemplars of any worthy trait would prove a valuable source of insights for those who want to emulate their triumphs. Why not literally play a game of "follow the leader" when we want to add to our repertoire of useful leadership ideas, attitudes, skills, and actions? We can't go far wrong asking ourselves what titans such as Alexander the Great, Julius Caesar, Abraham Lincoln, and George Washington would do, and then applying lessons learned from them to our own situation. Good examples are always worth our careful attention and our best efforts at emulation.

But our parents recognized that bad examples can be good too. "Don't do what they do, or you'll end up like them." Mothers and fathers have uttered that sentence, in many disguises, innumerable times throughout human history—their attempt to steer children away from "the wrong crowd." Indeed, what would parents do without a ready supply of failures, troublemakers, fools, and incompetents to use when showing their kids examples of what not to do?

---

1 John Charles Kunich is a tenured Professor of Law at Charlotte School of Law, Charlotte, North Carolina, where he also serves as Director of Research & Scholarship. He holds a Juris Doctor degree from Harvard Law School and is the author or co-author of five previous books and many scholarly articles. Dr. Richard I. Lester is Professor and Dean of Academic Affairs, Air University, Ira C. Eaker College for Professional Development, Maxwell Air Force Base, Alabama. He is the author of numerous scholarly articles and other books. Together, Kunich and Lester co-authored the book *Survival Kit for Leaders* (Skyward, 2003).

"Don't let that happen to you." It's a warning that packs much more punch when referring to an obvious illustration of the dire consequences befalling people who take the wrong turn in life. Failure personified is a more powerful motivator than abstract failure. When we can see for ourselves irrefutable evidence of the dreadful results, it's easier to grasp the point: Whatever you do, don't do what they did. Thus failure, in a sense, paves the highway to success...if we learn from mistakes. And if we can learn from the mistakes of others, we may not have to reenact every single mistake personally.

Can leaders with no particular connection to sports gain anything from reading a leadership book that takes baseball as its frame of reference? Either you are willing to consider that possibility, or you are about to put this book down forever, right now. Let's think about it. In baseball, as with anything else, failure should be seen as the opportunity to practice and improve; and failure is the name of the game you have to get past to win.

Effective leaders in all areas of endeavor understand that they will never be perfect—never "bat a thousand"—but they do try to learn something from every time they fail to connect. Success is not forever, and failure is not fatal for the optimistic—and realistic—leader. Too many people simply give up too easily. Good leaders keep the desire to forge ahead no matter what setbacks they suffer; and they understand that, to win, one must be able to take the bruises that come with the long street fight called life. They always look for ways to benefit from mistakes, including the vicarious lessons learned from other leaders' bad examples.

Although it is more polite to be positive, there is value not only in picking successful traits to copy, but also in identifying dangers to avoid. Like highway signs that run the gamut from the hopeful "Rest Area Next Right" to the cautionary "Dangerous Curve Ahead," our leadership lessons can and should be derived from extremes of both promise and peril. Good examples can add to our arsenal of usable tools, while bad examples subtract useless or even potentially fatal errors from our array of options. And if it can be as important to know what won't work as what will, there should be room to analyze outstanding examples of ineptitude. In baseball, as in any serious endeavor, leaders need to see farther, see more, and see differently if they are to move their teams to achieve greatness. They must search high and low, literally and figuratively, to learn the right lessons... and that includes outstanding examples of both success and failure.

That is the purpose of this book: To balance the scales just a bit, and place an extreme case of failure on the side opposite all those inspiring studies of history's greatest victors.

We don't write this from the standpoint of hard-hearted, cynical critics. Far from it, we have devoted many years in the vain hope that our subjects would reverse the curse of failure and at least prevail. Our decades of heartbreaking disappointment bear testimony of our qualifications to write this study. We have paid for each lesson as dearly as if we had committed the blunders ourselves. We offer these thoughts in the hope that something positive will emerge from all those years of tears.

The Chicago Cubs baseball team is the heart of this book. They are the only team to play continuously in the same city since the National League was created in 1876. We will draw from the Cubs' experience during the 100 years since their last World Series championship to develop a roadmap of hazards every leader needs to have at the ready. The Cubs' story is a rich and fascinating one, filled with great individual achievements, near misses, far misses, astounding collapses, head-shaking misjudgments, tantalizing partial successes, and wasted opportunities. We presume our readers possess some minimal level of Cubs background knowledge, which seems reasonable given the near-mythic status the Cubs have attained during the last century. However, a very brief summary is in order.

The Cubs last won the World Series and reigned as World Champions of baseball as recently as 1908. Teddy Roosevelt was still President of the United States; the federal income tax was only beginning to become a reality; and the hottest new car was the Ford Model T. Chicago's National League franchise has stood as a peculiar sort of "red light district" ever since, their traffic flow always stopping short of ultimate victory.

Cubs fans younger than, say, 110 years of age may not know it, but the Cubs were a veritable World Series fixture during the first few years of the Fall Classic's history. The World Series first began in 1903 to provide an annual showdown between the pennant winners from the venerable National League and the upstart new American League. After the initial experience in 1903, squabbles led to cancellation of the Series the following year before it resumed permanently in 1905.

It's hard to believe now, with the benefit of a century of hindsight, but the Cubs actually appeared in three of the first five World Series ever played, winning two of them! For three consecutive seasons (1906-1908) the Cubs were in the Series, falling to their cross-town rivals the White Sox in 1906, but then capturing back-to-back titles in 1907 and 1908. After a year's interlude in 1909, the Cubs made it back to the Series in 1910, but lost. Adding it all up, the Cubs appeared in four of the first seven World Series, and captured two crowns.

In the aftermath of their 1908 triumph, the Cubs initially did continue to win National League pennants with some regularity for the next four decades, finishing on top of their league in 1910, 1918, 1929, 1932, 1935, 1938, and 1945...but all without another World Series success. Following their World War II flirtation with glory, the Cubs then sank into a period of virtually unremitting wretchedness over the next 20-plus years, frequently occupying "the cellar" of the National League. They have not played so much as one World Series game since 1945—an interlude of more than 60 years. We need not remind you that many thousands of thick books have been filled with the countless events that have transpired since the end of the Second World War in 1945, but a World Series game featuring a Cubs team is not among them.

After two formal divisions within each league were introduced to baseball in 1969, and then three divisions per league in 1994, additional rounds of postseason baseball "playoffs" were created (first the League Championship Series, then joined by the Division Series as well) as prelude and prerequisite to playing in the World Series. During this era, the Cubs won their division in 1984, 1989, 2003, 2007, and 2008, and also made it to the Division Series as the "wild card" team in 1998. But the Cubs could never take their train all the way to the end of the line. They fell short of even reaching, let alone winning, the World Series each time, usually under emotionally wrenching circumstances. For their faithful and, needless to say, long-suffering fans, not only the final result but also the way in which it happened equaled the drama of a Shakespearean tragedy. It wasn't for nothing that political columnist George Will described his fellow Cubs' fans as "99.44 percent scar tissue."

Some good advice came from Babe Ruth, who unfortunately never played for the Cubs: "Never let the fear of striking out get in your way." To assure success, leaders must be persistent and keep their options open. They must leave their comfort zone and step into something undiscovered. And, as the Cubs have shown so many times, there is an endless variety of ways to win and to lose. In analyzing strategies for doing more of the former and less of the latter, it is helpful for leaders to ask two key questions: What exactly is our purpose? And what is our detailed, realistic plan to accomplish that purpose? The best leaders do exactly this.

However, the larger question asked in this book is: Where have all the leaders gone, and how have they allowed things to go so terribly off course? Our challenge: to use the Cubs' example, helping you answer this key question and develop into a better leader.

Good leaders are very much like the classic model of a Cubs fan: tough, disciplined, and committed. They see beyond the ivy-draped walls and on into the horizon, however distant and hard to find. Knowledge is the capacity for effective action in difficult situations, and leaders demand unparalleled access to information and ideas. But in today's hyper-competitive, rapidly evolving environment, leaders don't have the luxury of isolated, leisurely study, protracted experimentation, or making all the mistakes for themselves. They need to tap into the knowledge available from the mistakes of others...like the Cubs. We've written this book to help you gain additional insights into the issues involved in accomplishing this.

With the Boston Red Sox ending their 86-year World Series championship drought in 2004, and the Cubs' cross-town rival White Sox following suit in 2005 (88 years after their last title), the Cubs now are, beyond dispute, in a class by themselves. Snug, storied, ivy-walled Wrigley Field has been a no-fly zone for World Series flags longer than any other stadium, or any succession of stadiums. The centennial of the Cubs' last World Series crown arrived in 2008. A full century of losing should offer enough hard-knock lessons learned for anybody. It is appropriate, then, to select this triple-digit, major-milestone time for an analysis of what went wrong during the last ten decades...and what every leader can learn from this amazing and excruciating record. Our objective is to help you mine some life-changing lessons from the Cubs' rubble so that the teams you lead will enjoy much happier results. After all, there must be some consolation prize for Cubs fans in recompense for these many years of pain.

1st Inning
Individual Success Does Not Guarantee Team Victory

A losing team's stereotype is a collection of 100 percent complete incompetents, inept from top to bottom. This simplistic, cartoonish image probably never materializes in reality; and it certainly doesn't fit the many different Cubs teams that have played the game since 1908. The lack of a World Series championship has strangely coexisted with the presence—and even an abundance—of individual talent, often on the highest possible level. More than a few Cubs stars have earned baseball's most exalted personal honor, a place in the Hall of Fame at Cooperstown, New York. Yet they've never played on a world-champion team, or even a league pennant winner.

The Cubs' experience clearly confirms that even the best individual success is no guarantor of team victory. Leadership includes the ability to connect people, to figure out what's needed to build a winning team of complementary individual players, and then help get it done. Winning leaders are well grounded in the fundamentals of humility, and they try to impart that humility-based attitude to everyone on their team. They take far more pride in their people, staff, and organization than in any of their personal accomplishments. This is a key leadership lesson, but it can be difficult to apply within a star-struck institutional culture.

One could staff a hypothetical dream team of great players who amassed brilliant careers mostly or entirely as members of Cubs teams that have never won a World Series. The roster would include magical names such as Ernie Banks, Billy Williams, Ferguson Jenkins, Ron Santo, Ryne Sandberg, Gabby Hartnett, Billy Herman, Hack Wilson, Sammy Sosa, Mark Grace, and many others. The achievements of these and other standouts have won selection to all-star teams, most-valuable-player awards, batting championships, Cy Young awards, home-run titles, Gold Glove awards, and other enviable honors. But all these stars who tickled the ivy at Wrigley Field have never coalesced into a constellation of a World Championship. What went wrong?

Leaders must recognize that any team—any organization—requires more than exceptional individual talent and performance to reach the highest echelon of success. One Sosa can't switch a team from so-so to super, and he proved it during his glory years with the Cubs. During the 12 full seasons Sammy played for the Cubs after coming from the Texas Rangers, he compiled some remarkable achievements for an often sub-par team. In fact, over the entirety of the dozen-year Sosa era, during which he averaged an astonishing 45 homers per season, the Cubs lost significantly more games than they won. Here are his annual home-run totals and the Cubs' won-lost record for each year.

YEAR	SOSA'S HOMERS	CUBS' RECORD
1993	33	84 - 78
1994	25	49 - 64
1995	36	73 - 71
1996	40	76 - 86
1997	36	68 - 94
1998	66	90 - 73
1999	63	67 - 95
2000	50	65 - 97
2001	64	88 - 74
2002	49	67 - 95
2003	40	88 - 74
2004	35	89 - 73
TOTAL:	**537**	**904 - 974**

This chart illustrates some impressive anecdotal evidence regarding the relative importance of one star performer to his or her team's overall success. For example, during the five consecutive full seasons from 1998 through 2002, Sosa blasted an astounding 292 home runs, for a super-human *average* of 58.4 homers per year. During those same five other-worldly years, while Sosa was unleashing an unparalleled shower of power, his Cubs actually lost 57 more games than they won—an average annual deficit of more than 11 games. Even if we focus only on the breathtaking four-year rampage from 1998 through 2001, during which Sosa averaged more than 60 home runs each season, the Cubs could not manage to win as many games as they lost. The most staggering multi-year display of long-ball hitting by one player in baseball history failed to halt the Cubs' very different brand of staggering. The team as a collective unit had nothing to show for all of Sosa's record-smashing fireworks—except a single, very short-lived wild-card playoff fling in 1998.

Conversely, when the Cubs finally assembled a competent overall team of complementary talents to accompany Sosa's mega-muscle, the team as a whole performed much better, even though Sosa himself came back down to earth. The Cubs actually won their division in 2003 and nearly captured another wild-card berth in 2004. They finished with a combined 30 more wins than losses during those two years, despite relatively mere-mortal levels of home-run support from their big slugger (40 and 35 homers, respectively). Synergy, balance, leadership, and cooperation: These qualities made the Cubs much more successful overall than they had been during the previous five-year stretch when they mustered little support for the lone ex-Ranger as he performed his Babe Ruth act. What a difference a team makes.

Almost every aggregation of people at any given point in time can boast of a sprinkling of outstanding members, if only by random chance. These bright lights can be fun to watch, dazzling everyone with their ability. As with Sammy Sosa, their phenomenal performance might distract casual observers from the overall mediocrity of the larger whole. For a short time, stars can even carry the entire group on their backs, as heroes sometimes do. But life, like baseball, and like any team enterprise, is a long-term proposition. Over the course of a 162-game baseball season, a team needs more than a couple of big guns to consistently out-battle the competition.

Even more so, in business, government, academics, or everyday life, the long haul involves countless challenges, changing circumstances, unexpected obstacles, personal illness and injury, and formidable competitors ready and eager to exploit every advantage. No individual tower of strength can buttress the supporting structure's underlying weakness for more than a brief stretch.

The leader must assemble an organization that can and will work well together, with complementary skill sets, willingness to forsake personal glory for group success, and a unified vision. If this were easy, everyone would do it; but the leader must not be blinded by the flashy appeal of select individuals.

Star performers can, of course, be part of championship teams, but only part. They are not the team itself, nor are they more important than the larger entity, no matter what the agents say. Any team that allows its fortunes to be hijacked by the selfish pursuit of personal accomplishment will be doomed to internal conflict and ultimate failure. It takes great skill to identify the subtle, almost imperceptible talents and traits in each person—potential that can be refined and developed, meshing with other team members' skills to forge a harmonious organism-like unit. It's far easier to spot the headline-grabbing superstars, one at a time...but if this leads to neglect of overall team needs, the result will be an entertaining, losing team.

Outstanding individual performers can sometimes not only fail to lead their team to collective success, but can actually bring a net negative value to the larger organization. The same personality traits conducive to amassing impressive individual statistics and achievements often do not coexist with the characteristics that build group accomplishments. A star player might create tension between the desire to accumulate top-level personal victories and the team's broader needs.

Collective progress often depends on many people making plenty of personal sacrifices, quietly cooperating with others day after day, with little concern for where the credit lands. This selfless, behind the scenes, methodical focus on fundamentals tends to produce group results at the expense of illustrious individual achievement, which rests more on the single-minded pursuit of personal goals and honors.

Creating this kind of cooperative mutual altruism may be the most important function of leadership in developing winning teams. It's a lot more complex than just signing one famous superstar to a big, fat contract, and a lot more gradual and subtle. It also happens to be a lot more beneficial to the overall team.

As young children, we tended to believe in a fairy-tale world of princesses and princes, queens and kings, all with vast and unchallenged powers. We thought of being a leader as an unqualified blessing, amounting to getting our own way all the time, and calling all the shots. As realistic adults, we now know that such a top-down power monopoly is only found in a despotic dictator who rules with an iron fist, tightly clenched around a bundle of fear and force. Such selfish tyrants live and die by violence and threats, and their methods have no place in a modern free society...even though some megalomaniacs might imagine themselves as divine-right royalty within their little domains. But paradoxically, in our contemporary self-centered, "Me Century" culture, where narcissism and self-esteem are paramount, the best leaders put service to others before service to themselves. It seems that, to lead people who put themselves first, it is wise to stash our own egos in the recycling bin, and focus on what is best for our people, our organization, and our culture.

This concept of servant leadership is as old as humanity; but we are fated to re-learn it every generation. It feels backwards, as if the leader must put aside the crown's perquisites and privileges to stay on top...almost abdicating the throne to keep it. But authentic leadership is not about serving ourselves; and self-aggrandizement is foreign to the true leader. His or her proper aim is this: to move people to act for the greater good, not for the leader's petty and narrow personal interests. Only by regarding the broader interests of others—workers, colleagues, customers, society—can leaders prevail in a world where people routinely expect to be first.

Of course, over time a leader will strive to impart some measure of other-regarding selflessness to his or her employees as well, and move the entire organization into a service mode...but this plan unavoidably begins with the leader's own attitude. Thus, to pursue leadership as a service to others, and not as a position of status or power, will yield more productive results.

The concept and practice of servant leadership must live in both the head and the heart. Humility-based leaders are not concerned with power and control, but with support and facilitating effective activity. Good leaders are like quiet, invisible angels who lift us to our feet and guide us when our weary bodies feel unable to rise, walk, and run.

Humility is Kryptonite to the modern subspecies, *Homo sapiens narcissimus*, isn't it? For people weaned on an ego-rich, high self-esteem formula, humility and self-sacrifice would appear to be an oxymoron—a concept so blatantly at odds with itself, it's as moronic as an ox.

But that is precisely why humility is so crucial to productive leadership. It isn't easy, and it isn't obvious, but it is effective. We must turn outside our constricted, selfish, "Yea, me!" mini-world, and look at what is best for others. Only then can we truly serve them and, ultimately, succeed in our own right. A dictator might demand that his serfs raise his huge statue in the city square; but one day that monument to megalomania will be torn down, maybe by those same serfs. The only lasting memorials to leaders are those earned through assiduous devotion to something greater than the leader, and greater than any one person. Leaders are driven by a higher purpose and an absolute commitment to achieving that purpose.

For better or—you guessed it—for worse, the Cubs have very often featured a serious deficiency of this humility-infused leadership. Their bumper crop of narcissists has seldom been leavened with an adequate sprinkling of humble, other-oriented leaders; and this is one reason for the team's seemingly endless "temporary" slump.

The Cubs would have been better served by a few more hard-playing, fundamentally solid, do-the-little-things-right players along the lines of Billy Herman (with the team during the 1930s) and Glenn Beckert (1960s and early 1970s). Herman and Beckert had none of the slugging power usually (over)emphasized by Cubs teams; but they worked tirelessly to master game-winning fine points such as the sacrifice bunt, the hit-and-run, avoiding strikeouts, hitting behind the runner to advance men into scoring position, and delivering a key sacrifice fly. Their personal statistics weren't eye-popping, but they quietly, consistently, and reliably did more to help their team win than a limousine full of boom-or-bust, all-out hard swingers. They led by example, with both humility and inspiration. It wasn't their fault so few of their teammates were paying attention.

That splendid brand of selfless leadership differs greatly from the "best friend" or babysitter leadership—the kind you might think appropriate for workers coddled, pampered, and cushioned with an inflated sense of self-esteem since conception. It does no one any favors to dumb down the organization's expected performance level, or to numb down our alertness for failure to meet those expectations.

Authentic leadership is all about recognizing the truth about ourselves, our co-workers, our competitors, our customers, and our culture—and then insisting on a cooperative and coordinated approach to making that truth work for our organization. You can't do this with sloppy work, lowered standards, tolerance for intolerable attitudes, or excuses for inexcusable behavior. People will eventually respond positively and appropriately to a selfless leader who settles for nothing less than best efforts and high-quality production from everyone—the leader to the most inexperienced newcomer.

Hydroponically grown, nanny-cosseted self-esteem junkies will probably bristle initially when someone suggests (for maybe the first time in their lives) that their performance is less than above average. But once it becomes clear that no-excuse, no-kidding production is demanded from everyone, including the leader, the junkies too will usually adapt. They'll even take pride in at last meeting and exceeding exacting standards.

After all, self-esteem is only selfish steam unless there is real substance behind it; and undeserved praise is ultimately seen as saccharine for the soul. As generations of recruits have learned the hard way from surviving a grueling boot camp, we derive great value from reaching deep within to overcome the steepest life challenges. Genuine pride and camaraderie, rising from personal and organizational triumph, far outshines any false pride handed out by well-meaning but overly lenient caregivers. Earned rewards and accolades prove infinitely more satisfying, precisely because we had to toil, think, struggle, and do more in order to obtain them. In that sense, the gift of high standards and high expectations for one and all remains one of the greatest and truest gifts any leader can convey.

All for One and One for All

When your team needs just one run to win, and you are at bat with a runner on third base and less than two out, you do the team no favors by swinging with all your might. A home run is not what your team needs. When you strike out trying for that home run, you fail to get the humble ground ball or sacrifice fly that would have helped your team.

But players who hit a lot of homers will get big, lucrative contracts and loads of adoring fans, while players who do the "little things" that help their teams win may not collect such jaw-dropping numbers. Players who give up a chance for a big, showy hit to do what the situation actually calls for (such as hitting behind the runner, taking a couple of strikes, bunting, lofting a sacrifice fly, or just making contact with the ball) are thinking of their team's needs, placing their mates above their own personal statistics.

It is much the same in business, government, and other lines of endeavor. Certain activities bring individual accolades, rewards, and glory, while other less-conspicuous pursuits prove ultimately more important to the organization's overall good. Powerful incentives in every system appeal to our selfish and self-centered impulses, telling us to do what's best for our own career, our own performance reports, and our own professional resume.

We might even delude ourselves with the notion that what's best for us is also what's best for our organization in the long run; and so we are truly team players by pressing for those individual prizes. But co-workers can tell when their fellows only fend for themselves. Loners invariably choose to build their own numbers when a conflict arises between collective and personal interests. They will not be among those volunteering to work long, difficult hours when no prospect exists for individual glorification and gratification.

A star in any setting must actively resist the temptation to become a prima donna, because the money and positive publicity are so attractive and addictive. But as generations of Cubs teams have shown, such temptations too often prove irresistible. The stars begin expecting and even demanding the freedom, perquisites, and special benefits commensurate with their exalted status.

Leaders must ensure that the same set of rules applies to everyone, with no preferential treatment for prima donnas regardless of their achievements. Few things harm an organization more than an environment in which some people are allowed to flout the rules and flaunt a privileged stature, whether by virtue of whom they know or what they've done. Such a double standard splinters a team into at least two factions—the haves and have nots—and breeds a culture of divisiveness, unfairness, disunity, inequality, and disparate treatment.

There are many examples of a single, brilliant performer becoming a detriment to his team, despite or because of his enormous talent. Some of the greatest players in baseball history have been known as disruptive influences on their own team, through a combination of selfishness, egotism, insistence on preferential treatment, arrogance, disregard for rules, failure to connect with teammates, disdain for others' feelings, and refusal to participate in the usual practice sessions.

Icons such as Barry Bonds, Ty Cobb, Rogers Hornsby, and Dick Allen at times indulged themselves in a star mentality. Their managers often found themselves unable or ill-equipped to impose uniform standards on such exceptional individuals. Over time, this pulled their teams apart. Paradoxically, some of the most magnificent talents of all time actually caused so much team damage that many believed they were, on balance, a liability instead of an asset. Rather than forming the solid foundation around which a well-balanced winning team could be carefully assembled, they factionalized and divided it.

Good leaders understand that where there is unity, there is strength… and where there is division, there is weakness. Effective leaders strive for organizational unity. Teamwork is key. Lou Holtz modeled this when he went to the University of Minnesota as head football coach. He passed out T-shirts at his first meeting with his players. In large block letters read the word **TEAM**; in tiny letters below: **me**. Some of the biggest stars can't buy that, and see only their own names up in lights.

Life is a team effort, not just a jumble of selfish, independent island-individuals obsessed with their own personal advancement. No one in either the organizational or personal world gets very far alone, except along the trail to irrelevance. Effective organizations and their leaders need dedicated people who work as a coordinated matrix, and who support, encourage, and inspire mutual accomplishment.

To combat the centrifugal tendency exerted on many star-struck teams, Cubs Fan leaders must be scrupulously uniform in applying the same rules to everyone. They must diligently seek out and publicly reward the less obvious, but very important, cooperative efforts their people contribute to group success. This requires an ample supply of courage, insight, diplomacy, and communication skill on the part of the leader "blessed" with extraordinarily talented problem children, and a larger number of ordinary workers who might be willing to give an extra effort. Prima-donna stars are amply rewarded by the system already, because even casual observers can easily notice such gaudy feats, and will pay handsomely to encourage more of the same. But unless the leader makes the extra effort to discover and incentivize below-the-radar teamwork, there's no reason to expect it to proliferate on its own.

It is too easy for leaders to look only for the splashy, can't-miss-it success stories when it comes to recognizing and compensating people for their good work. It may be effortless to join the crowd and dole out plaudits for the headline-makers. But it proves counterproductive if it comes at the expense of the subtle, selfless, basic, big-picture, cooperative efforts of a greater number of "average" workers. Just as the Cubs haven't won when they've boasted a line-up overflowing with all-stars, any organization will fall short if it stresses one-by-one personal glory, and neglects the humility-infused synergy that brings team success.

Leaders must be astute judges of what does and does not count toward collective progress. They must be brave enough to show prima donnas to the door unless they put the group's interests above their personal careerism. Those countless little examples of mutual cooperation, sparkling in the background, are the seeds of the future; leaders have to do what it takes to become aware of them, nurture them, reward them, and encourage others to emulate them.

The Cubs' century of sad but star-lit nights shows that we do not need great leaders or great star performers. We need teachable, flexible, diligent leaders who can build effective teams from people with good fundamental talents...leaders who will bring out the latent greatness in all of them. Neither the leader nor the followers have to be brilliant, phenomenally talented, dazzlingly charismatic, or any other grab-bag of superlatives pulled from a thesaurus. Organizational excellence does not have its roots in the extremes of the few, but rather in the solid attributes of the many, and in the way they cooperate, synergize, and balance. And that's very good news for the 99.999 percent of us who aren't superstars.

In fact, here's a final disadvantage of the star system: its surprisingly deleterious impact on overall team effectiveness in terms of actual aggregate productivity. The over-reliance on one or two people, regardless of stellar quality, usually renders the whole team very vulnerable to injuries, slumps, or other loss. If those key performers become unavailable or temporarily ineffective (as do even the greatest standouts in any field) the entire team's fortunes are disproportionately affected. Though it may seem illogical that a team can be hurt by the presence of one or two superstars, this is one more example of how that can indeed happen when leaders succumb to the temptation to rely too heavily on the big names. The imbalance this forces upon the entire unit drags down everyone, despite—or more accurately, because of—the stars and the way the leader handles them.

When the leader over-stresses an elite core's value, everyone who is not a "star" becomes (and quite understandably feels) just part of the supporting cast, one of the proverbial "little people," of less importance and of less usefulness. This makes it easier for opponents to overwhelm the team by working around or avoiding the few strong points, hammering the many neglected weak and vulnerable spots. Meanwhile, the team itself finds it difficult to form a united coalition, in light of the disparities and inequalities within its own ranks.

In baseball, even the greatest starting pitcher, such as the Cubs' famed Ferguson Jenkins, usually can only work every fourth or fifth day. So what happens the rest of the time if too many resources have been lavished on that one person? Jenkins was a marvelous pitcher—a tremendous workhorse who often pitched complete-game victories, and led the league in innings pitched. He achieved the amazing milestone of winning 20 or more games for the Cubs in six consecutive seasons…but he never learned how to clone himself, and even he couldn't pitch every game. A 20-game winner like Fergie is at the very pinnacle of his profession; but it usually takes more than four times that many victories for a baseball team to contend for a championship in any given season. A team that wins only one-fourth of its games, or anywhere near that fraction, always dwells in the cellar.

Likewise, think about a lineup with only one productive slugger, such as the Cubs during the immortal Ernie Banks' splendid MVP years—the late 1950s and early 1960s. If ever a player were capable of carrying a team all alone it was Banks, the masterful power-hitting shortstop. He was able to turn a double-play in the top of an inning, then in the bottom half smash a homer into Waveland Avenue traffic beyond Wrigley Field's bleachers. But even with a Hall-of-Fame hitter at his glorious peak, the Cubs were easy pickings for other teams that simply refused in key spots to give "Mr. Cub" anything good to hit. Other teams often pitched around Ernie and even intentionally walked him when the game was on the line, while taking advantage of all the weak hitters batting before and after him.

Baseball is a team sport, and not even the most wonderful individual performer can single-handedly carry a group that fails to build a strong, well-balanced, overall squad matrix, and find a way to use every member optimally. Ernie Banks, ever the cheerful optimist, was known for saying, "Let's play two today!" But without an adequate mutual-support system around him, playing two games often meant doubleheader losses for the Cubs.

The Wrigley-based clubs have often attempted to construct entire winning teams on top of only one large pillar, and that is no way to establish a firm foundation, only a see-saw.

The same is true for every organization consisting of more than one person. A single star might look good when it shines, but it can't light up the whole sky, or do much to fire the imagination when only empty space surrounds it; that's why we have no one-star constellations. Outstanding talents can be a blessing for any group, but only if those talents blend with the right mixture of complementary assets...and a shared collective understanding that no isolated component is indispensable, nor is any insignificant.

1st Inning Discussion Questions

1. Have you ever been in an organization where one or more "star performers" appeared exempt from the usual rules? How did this affect the team as a whole? What could the leaders have done to improve the situation?

2. Does the amount of money involved in professional sports today make it more difficult or less difficult for front-office and on-the-field leaders to deal with challenges? In what way does money change the leader's range of options?

3. Should top-performing employees be singled out for additional pay, status, and/or official recognition? Why or why not?

4. How should leaders reward and incentivize outstanding work without fostering the "star system" and inviting accusations of double standards and favoritism?

5. How well does your organization provide a positive correlation between compensation/benefits and value added by workers at all levels? What could be done to create a better match between pay and performance?

6. What would you do in your line of work when you must compete against an organization that features one or two brilliant performers?

7. How does your approach differ when your main competitor skillfully integrates the complementary assets and weaknesses of the entire unit?

8. To what extent is a prima donna's selfish, privileged attitude the self-proclaimed star's fault? What role can a leader play in either facilitating or mitigating this divisive self-centeredness?

9. In the military, there is an old saying that "rank has its privileges." Does someone earn special privileges by virtue of extended service and/or exceptional productivity?

10. How can you differentiate between morale-splitting preferential treatment and effective incentives to reward outstanding work? How can a leader help his or her team appreciate the differences?

2nd Inning

Don't Count Your Pennants Before They're Won

How have the Cubs managed to stay away from the World Series since 1945? How could the Cubs play for six decades without a trip to the Fall Classic, while cold wars, hot wars, and streams of America's presidents came and went? Suffice it to say it wasn't pretty. They have used two very different methods of long-term Series avoidance, to which we will return in greater detail in our 6th Inning. For sake of our present discussion, however, we want to introduce the main concepts here.

The Cubs' predominant paradigm has been to lose early and often, and thus remain consistently at or near the pile's bottom all along, so distant from the top only one question remained: Would any other team finish the season with a worse record? This "lose big" pattern offers one significant advantage—disappointment, heartbreak, and pressure are kept to a minimum. Later in this book, we will give this particular mode of losing another name: the bottom scraper. No one stays under the radar like a bottom scraper; and at various points in time the Cubs have limped along for year after year, losing with remarkable regularity, and scarcely attracting anyone's notice.

The other way to steer clear of success proves much more painful, although it comes with tantalizing attractions. On several unforgettable occasions (and how we've tried to forget them!) the Cubs have performed very well during most of the season, only to fall short at the threshold of glory. This entails a more complicated roadmap to ruin, with some dramatic U-turns and sharp curves. This ride can be much more interesting than the straight line to last place. The good times are nice while they last, but the whiplash from sudden crashes can be extremely traumatic.

It is very painful for us to recount in detail the Cubs' most glaring examples of late-season and postseason meltdowns. Years of therapy could easily be undone by the attempt to unearth memories better left buried under thick layers of denial. Suffice it to say that every Cubs fan knows the story by heart—and by heartbreak. It is more than enough to mention the most infamous years: 1945, 1969, 1984, 1989, 2003, and 2004. If you don't know what happened during each of those seasons to block the Cubs' path to a World Series triumph, we're sorely tempted (and we do mean sorely) to ask you to look it up for yourself.

Oh, all right. We'll put our mental health on the line and exhume an example or two right now. Later in this book, we will try to summon up enough courage to discuss other horrors from this litany of catastrophes in a little more depth. If this exercise in masochism hands us a lifetime ticket on the Disoriented Express, at least you can comfort yourself with this thought: The money you paid for this volume will help cover the cost of a blue-ribbon team of Austrian psychiatrists for the authors.

Probably the most notorious case comes from 1969, a vintage year for Cubs' bad examples. The Cubs began the '69 season playing like champions right from Opening Day, jumping to a sizable lead over their closest competitors. Millions of fans soon joined in the carnival atmosphere generated by the uncommon taste of early success. After all, in 1969 the Cubs had not played a single game of post-regular-season baseball in 24 years (since the 1945 World Series), and it seemed to be about time.

Jack Brickhouse had been their enthusiastic and cheerful broadcast announcer for many lean years with little to cheer about, beginning in the late 1940s. Now he delighted in yelling his trademark home run call "Hey-Hey!" as the Cubs' long blasts came at long last in bunches. Capitalizing on their new-found success, the Cubs actually released a record album, including a song integrating Brickhouse's famous battle cry: "Hey-Hey! Holy mackerel! No doubt about it! The Cubs are on their way!" The tune may not have made Beethoven roll over, but we can imagine Joe Tinker, Johnny Evers, and Frank Chance performing posthumous flips—their spirits recalling the Cubs 1907 and 1908 World Series championships— their last, accomplished before the era of modern sound recordings.

Even Ron Santo, the Cubs' veteran slugging third baseman and a proven star, got caught up in the party mentality. Well before the season was even half over, Santo started performing a unique ritual at the conclusion of every Cubs win at home. When each game ended in a Cubs triumph, Santo dashed down the left-field foul line toward the Cubs' clubhouse. As he ran, Santo would leap in the air and click his heels multiple times in a type of victory dance—the foot version of chest thumping. It was an ostentatious in-your-face display to a degree rarely seen in the baseball world, especially in the more reserved climate of professional baseball in 1969.

Cubs fans soon came to expect Santo to repeat his heel-clicking sprint after every win, and they cheered wildly in appreciation as he obliged them. Meanwhile opposing teams fumed at being humiliated so brazenly, and they gained additional motivation to beat the braggart Cubs next time. Ultimately, when the Cubs at last plummeted out of first place in September, Santo's antics quietly ended, along with hopes of a long-delayed World Series for Chicago. This defeat was especially bitter, because Santo and the Cubs were forced to tacitly admit the foolishness and false bravado of his heel-clicking act.

Another crushing example of the disastrous effects of prematurely assuming victory came 15 baseball seasons later. The year 1984 has long had Orwellian connotations, and the Cubs did their part to reinforce those strangely mixed messages. Unexpectedly competitive that year, the Cubs found themselves in contention for a pennant. Their beloved folk-hero broadcaster, Harry Caray, sprinkled his on-the-air commentary with ecstatic shouts of "Holy cow!" after every Cubs homer, and "Cubs win!" after each victory. With a mostly-veteran lineup, led by superlative second baseman Ryne Sandberg and solid pitching sparked by mid-year acquisition Rick Sutcliffe, the wins piled up. It was decidedly unfamiliar territory for the Cubs, and they liked it. They even came to expect it.

It should have been an unmistakable danger signal when Chicago singer-songwriter Steve Goodman wrote the anthem "Go, Cubs, Go!" early in 1984 to celebrate his team's march to glory. Goodman sang, "This is the year and the Cubs are real," having what it takes "to be the best in the National League." Echoes of the 1969 tune "Hey-Hey! Holy Mackerel!" reverberated in the ears of everyone who heard "Go, Cubs, Go!" Goodman went as far as to include several current Cubs players (among them Gary Matthews, Jody Davis, and Keith Moreland) in the recording as back-up singers.

The Cubs seemed to be a team of destiny in 1984. In one late-season game, they were narrowly ahead in the final inning with enemy runners on base and their ace relief pitcher, Lee Smith, trying to get the last two outs. The batter walloped one of Smith's pitches right back up the middle, a screaming line drive. It looked like a certain hit. But it struck Smith on the shoulder and caromed, on the fly, to Cubs shortstop Larry Bowa who caught the ball in mid-air. Bowa fired the ball to first to complete a freakish game-ending double play. At this, Harry Caray yelled with the voice of the Cubs and their fans everywhere, "Cubs win! Cubs win! What a lucky break! The Good Lord wants the Cubs to win!" Sadly, subsequent events would expose Harry's prophetic gifts as less than infallible.

For a long time it appeared that Harry might be right. The regular season thrived with thrilling moments that, for many players and fans, created a giddy sensation: the inevitability of the Cubs as the next World Champions. One unforgettable example came against the Cardinals at Wrigley Field on June 23, to this day still referred to as "the Sandberg game." Batting against the nearly unhittable Hall-of-Fame reliever (and former Cub) Bruce Sutter, Ryne Sandberg did what many believed to be the impossible. Sandberg hit consecutive game-tying home runs off Sutter in both the 9th and 10th innings. His game total of seven runs batted in and five hits led the Cubs, astonishingly, to an eventual 12-11 victory in 11 innings. For Chicago, 1984 was that kind of year...up to a point.

Steve Goodman, the composer of "Go, Cubs, Go!" succumbed to cancer on September 20, four days before the Cubs clinched first place in their division. For some fans it was too cruel to accept, especially in light of another song Goodman had written only one year earlier, "A Dying Cub Fan's Last Request." In that poignant ballad, Steve sang of the Cubs' stealing his youth and how they would "raise up a young boy's hopes and then just crush 'em like so many paper beer cups." Had he lived only three weeks longer he would have witnessed his words proved prophetic.

The Cubs won their division with the best record in the National League, and faced the San Diego Padres in a best-three-out-of-five playoff series to decide the pennant. It was the first time the Cubs had been in any championship playoff or World Series in 39 years, dating back to 1945. They were eager to claim the prize that had been so cruelly denied them in 1969.

The first two games of the playoffs were in Wrigley Field, and the Cubs won both of them. In fact, they crushed the Padres behind ace starter Rick Sutcliffe in Game One, 13-0. The Cubs homers flew out of the park, and even fleet leadoff batter Bob Dernier and Sutcliffe himself joined the home-run parade. The Cubs easily won Game Two as well, led by another excellent pitching performance from Steve Trout. As the series moved to San Diego, many Cubs firmly agreed with Harry Caray that divine intervention had finally guaranteed the Cubs a trip to the World Series. After all, the Cubs needed to win just one more game out of the possible three remaining to get to the promised land.

During the long flight to California, Larry Bowa and a couple of the other Cubs veterans with playoff experience became concerned that their teammates were overconfident. Bowa worried that too many Cubs considered their victory a foregone conclusion. He knew, from his years of experience with the Philadelphia Phillies, all about the dangers of overconfidence and taking success for granted. But many of his fellow Cubs lacked that wisdom. Would they have to learn their lessons the hard way?

Events would soon prove that the Cubs had indeed assumed their pennant to be in the bag a bit too early. The Padres swept all three of the remaining games, and once again sent the Cubs home to watch the World Series on television. The last two of these games were very close, tension-filled, and fertile ground for second-guessers. The Cubs and their fans were shocked when the Padres took Game Four 7-5 on Steve Garvey's two-run walk-off homer in the bottom of the 9th against Cubs closer Lee Smith. The Cubs in that game had twice fought back to overcome two-run deficits, only to see the game suddenly torn from them at the end. But incredibly, Game Five the next day, October 7, was even more excruciating.

Even with the series tied at two games apiece in the aftermath of the Padres' back-to-back victories, the Cubs still fully expected to win it all. They knew in their hearts that 1984 was their year, as Steve Goodman sang in "Go, Cubs, Go!" In part, this seemed justified, because Sutcliffe was pitching again. He had won 16 games and lost only one during the regular season, and seemed invincible. Earlier in the playoff series, in Game One, he had stopped the Padres cold with his arm and his bat. Plus, the Cubs began Game Five on fire, jumping out to an early 3-0 lead on homers by Leon Durham and Jody Davis. Meanwhile, Sutcliffe was in top form, mowing down the Padres as usual. He allowed no runs on only two hits during the first five innings, and all was right with the Cubs world. Everything was proceeding according to the foreordained pro-Cubs opera, with lyrics by Steve Goodman.

But the Padres chipped away with two runs off Sutcliffe in the 6th inning. Then in the 7th inning the entire season broke to pieces. The Padres scored four runs to take a lead they never relinquished. Carmelo Martinez, a former Cub, began the inning by drawing a walk from Sutcliffe on four pitches. He moved to second on a sacrifice bunt, and then scored the tying run when a sharp grounder by pinch-hitter Tim Flannery went right through first baseman Leon Durham's legs for an incredible, unforgettable error. It was then the Cubs stopped believing that miracles were due only to them. The incident became known in Cubs lore as the "Gatorade Glove Play," because some of the thirst-quenching beverage had been spilled on Durham's glove in the dugout between innings. Only in Chicago could Gatorade seriously be accused of making major league gloves repel baseballs. Who knew?

In any event, a few moments later Tony Gwynn hit a hard smash toward Gold-Glove winning second baseman Ryne Sandberg. It looked like an automatic double-play ball with the immortal Sandberg ready to field it. But the ball suddenly took a bad hop and flew over Sandberg's shoulder. The double play was instantly transformed into a two-run double. The pennant that the Cubs, as a matter of divine right had long considered their own, would fly in San Diego instead.

When everything is going well for the Cubs, as it was during most of 1969 and 1984, and the team is riding high on a giddy surge of success, it is easy to count the National League pennant as already won. Why not begin at the earliest opportunity the happy task of planning for the inevitable and long-awaited World Series in Wrigley Field?

Fans, players, managers, and team executives alike are susceptible to this pleasant delusion. It's certainly understandable that they are eager to declare victory prematurely, because so many decades (not just years, decades) have elapsed since the Cubs even made it to a World Series, let alone won it. Who wouldn't love to get rid of all the talk of curses and failure and move on to the Elysian plains of bragging rights and glory? This penchant for anticipatory celebration becomes most acute when the team is far ahead of its closest rivals with only a few weeks left in the season (as in 1969), or one playoff victory away from the pennant and a trip to the Series…and even leading in that last game with only a few outs to go (as in 1984 and 2003). Oh, the humanity!

From the standpoint of the actual players and manager, there is another dangerous facet of prematurely assuming victory. Once performers start counting their current challenges as already overcome, they often change the way they approach the tasks still at hand. They shift focus to the next phase, such as the division series, league championship series, or World Series, damaging their ability to no-kidding win the contest they're still involved in.

This change can take several forms, some of them deliberate and others subconscious. For example, the manager might juggle the pitching rotation, setting it up for maximum benefit during the next phase of competition, often by giving key pitchers an extra day of rest or even skipping a scheduled starting assignment. Similarly, players with nagging injuries could be allowed to take several games off so as to be in peak form for the coming series, even though they currently are capable of playing well.

Manager and players alike can tend to lose some of their aggressiveness, and begin coasting along on auto-pilot—not the style of performance that brought them to the front yard of success in the first place. Players might take fewer chances in the field or on the base paths, for fear of suffering an injury that would disable them during the anticipated future stages of competition. They no longer dive for balls they ordinarily would try their hardest to catch, or run full-speed when they hit a ground ball, or attempt to steal a base in a close game, or go from first to third base on a single. It all adds up to a play-it-safe attitude. Once it takes hold of a team, it can be very difficult to scrape it off and resume the previous full-throttle competitiveness when crunch time arrives. Teams don't easily shift gears from ferocious to cautious and back again.

Through all of these well-explored pitfalls, the Cubs have injected new meaning into this venerable cliché: "Don't count your chickens before they're hatched." It's obvious why the Cubs and their fans would be a bit overeager to declare victory, having endured such a protracted dry spell. But losing hurts all the more when we've already begun celebrating a win, and premature declarations of victory can invigorate lurking competitors.

The lesson for leaders is deceptively simple, and thus easy to miss. Although it is important to plan ahead and be prepared for further challenges still to come, this is an absolute prerequisite: Make sure that all necessary intervening steps have been definitively secured. Any leader that neglects this essential principle is running full-speed at a brick wall disguised as an ivy cushion. No one can graduate from good to great without preliminarily doing what it takes to become good. No one receives an advanced degree without earning a high-school diploma and an undergraduate degree first. And no one wins the World Series without winning their league's championship along the way.

In our own careers, it can be tempting to think one or two promotions or assignments ahead, pleasantly imagining our unbroken string of future triumphs paving our highway to higher glory. These dreams, however, are fated to remain just dreams unless they are carefully rooted in hard reality, with plenty of patience, foundation-laying, and attention to the myriad mundane details that litter the landscape between our goals and our present situation. It's fine to be a visionary, but even visionaries cannot long take their eyes off the immediate tasks at hand, lest they trip over solid and unyielding stumbling blocks while gazing at the horizon. A leader's fantasy of herself in the Big Boss's chair must be buttressed with less heady, but more headachy, work on all the things that need to be accomplished as part of her present position. Failure there guarantees that someone else will win the race to the top.

Yes, it can be boring and tedious to concentrate on all the day-to-day details that add up to doing the job we now have. Yes, it is natural to be impatient for greater challenges and loftier rewards. But the Cubs have repeatedly taught us this excruciating lesson: Those who take their eyes off the ball in front of them never get to hold the big trophy. For many Cub fans, winning the big trophy has been so rare that life seems like a gleam of light between two eternities.

When we count our pennants before they're won, we succumb to the tendency to coast, to get sloppy, and neglect fundamentals. Healthy confidence ossifies into arrogance and disdain for our competition, leading us to underestimate them, and let them take the initiative. Although planning is indispensable to success, too much planning in the form of looking forward to future challenges, to the neglect of each day's mundane chores, causes staleness, going through the motions, and lack of aggressiveness as we slide toward presumptive glory. Rather than concentrating on accomplishing our current goals and objectives "just in time" with attention to all the pertinent details, we mentally skip ahead to the good stuff we expect to come our way, and trip over no-kidding, present-day reality.

We're of no earthly good if we're always keeping our head in the clouds. We focus too much on how we'll celebrate *when* we win, and not enough on what we will do every day *to* win. We naturally keep our eyes on the scoreboard and not on the ball, because we are so determined to win that ultimate prize we've been working toward for such a long time.

Unfortunately, that is a time-tested method of falling out of first place. If your focus is on the ball, the scoreboard will take care of itself.

We lose our competitive edge when we allow ourselves to assume we've got it made. We think, "Why mess with success? If it ain't broke..." It all adds up to stand-pat complacency and a lack of continuous self-evaluation and readjustment. When we assume that it's in the bag, we become too cautious, too risk-averse, and let others set the agenda. We relinquish the aggressiveness and proactive willingness to take calculated risks that lifted us to the top in the first instance. Instead of having it in the bag, we wind up in the bag.

There is also an element of insecurity blended with premature assumption of victory. Scoreboard obsession is about more than just our confident wish to confirm our continued success. In part we also tend to watch the scoreboard because we're looking over our shoulders, concerned with how the competition is doing. This violates Satchel Paige's axiom, "Don't look back; something might be gaining on you." We become afraid to make an error, and grow too tense and tentative, as if in subconscious recognition that we might still blow it all.

Paradoxically, our over-confidence can breed weakness. As soon as we take victory for granted, there is also the fear of collapse, choking, folding in the clutch—especially where we have a history of doing it before. Ghosts haunt us, old curses taunt us, improbable blunders take on inordinate significance, and we begin anxiously looking for signs of another end-game implosion. Past can easily become prologue under such conditions.

Leadership must step up to the plate and maintain focus for the entire organization. If the leader frequently reminds each team member precisely what he or she must do on a short-term, middle-term, and long-term basis, this will lower the risk of lost perspective. But leaders are themselves prone to losing sight of the immediate task at hand as they strive to think strategically and plan for challenges to come. So it is vital that leaders devote some time each day to reviewing current and near-term hurdles.

Clearly, a lack of "clear line of sight" leadership has been a key element contributing to problems the Cubs have encountered since 1945. Leaders, because of their vision and determination to make a positive difference, can see things that others do not see, and hear things that others miss. Successful leaders continually reassess the situation, adapting to changed circumstances. They remain vigilant to the dangers of just copying their own past successes, or unthinkingly repeating the techniques that have worked for others. Why? Because they know that no imitation was ever a masterpiece. Until final triumph, every enterprise is always a work in progress. Mid-course adjustments are good, but true success requires re-evaluation and prudent adjustments at every stage.

There is another facet to the type of unfocused leadership that prematurely assumes victory. What if the organization lacks a strong leader, or there is a dearth of clarity as to who is really at the helm? The Cubs again have provided us with a classic example—a real-world, two-year experiment in chaos theory. Pay attention, because we will probably never see the likes of this again, for reasons that will soon become abundantly clear.

During the 1961 and 1962 baseball seasons, Cubs owner Philip K. Wrigley instituted a novel approach to on-the-field management. He didn't have a manager. Or, more accurately, he had several. The idea was for the Cubs to be led by a rotating "College of Coaches," where the entire coaching staff took turns as "head coach," each serving for a few weeks before moving over for the next coach. It was management by committee, with no one person in charge overall for more than a brief period at a time. The College of Coaches consisted of four individuals in 1961, and three in 1962.

What was the result of this creative exercise in leaderless leadership? In 1960, just before the advent of the College of Coaches, the Cubs finished next to last (seventh in an eight-team league), with 60 wins and 94 losses. Under the collectivist experiment in 1961, the Cubs again wound up next to last, amassing 64 victories and 90 defeats. The National League expanded to 10 teams in 1962, the second and final year of the College of Coaches, and the Cubs once again came in next to last, this time ninth in a 10-team league, finishing even lower than the first-year team from Houston, with a record of 59 wins against 103 losses. As the Cubs returned to one-person management in 1963, the team showed considerable improvement, ending up seventh out of 10 teams, with a won-lost mark of 82 and 80. The lesson was obvious, even to the Cubs' senior management: As there is one body, so can there be but one head that is ultimately responsible for everything, including helping others to become leaders.

The Cubs' experiment in round-robin, follow-the-leader egalitarianism was widely judged a failure, and, not surprisingly, it has never been replicated. One might argue that you can't do much worse than the Cubs did, with or without a leader, during the three years from 1960 through 1962, but it appeared that the College of Coaches wasn't doing anything to improve team performance either. When no one is truly in charge, and everyone knows that in short order there will be a new person in the big chair, it is impossible to build stability, continuity, and a consistent approach. There is no buck-stops-here accountability that rests permanently and identifiably with one leader, so no one is truly accountable for what happens. Bad leaders are certainly capable of driving a team into the ground, but without any leaders at all the team will never get off the ground in the first place.

The Cubs flirtation with the College of Coaches demonstrates the need for strong leadership to establish, adjust, and maintain team priorities. Without this leadership, people will tend to jump to the wrong conclusions, prematurely declare victory (or defeat), and generally lose sight of the collective vision.

In this connection, leaders are able to hear the music of tomorrow while having the courage to learn all the steps to the dance today. They keep their focus on the vision, on what they want their team to be, and break down the long-term grand plan into manageable everyday bite-sized pieces. This necessarily includes the leader's ability to create a clear line of sight for each member of the team, enabling everyone to know what's required at every stage, and to see the impact of his or her contribution. This type of consistent, coordinated leadership needs someone to take firm hold of the steering wheel, keep both eyes on the road ahead, and drive—not just a merry-go-round of temps taking turns at sitting in the driver's seat.

Given that it is dangerous to prematurely take victory for granted, what can a leader do to decide which risks are worth proactive attention? Let's look at a particularly useful tool that can help a leader deal constructively with potential hazards that might lie between present success and future achievement.

A leader can make more rational decisions regarding the amount of attention due worst-case scenarios, and other strategic planning puzzles, by applying some variant of "Pascal's Wager"—a useful method of logically assessing the optimal decision leaders should make, given the multiple and enormous unknowns inherent in many difficult problems. As every leader understands, vast unknown and unknowable gaps exist in the pertinent facts which aid any rational person when determining a course of action.

Blaise Pascal (1623-1662) was a brilliant French mathematician, scientist, and philosopher. His famous "wager" is one of the most intriguing of his many contributions. In its original form, Pascal's Wager deals with our choice of whether to believe in God; or more accurately, our decision whether to believe in God and to live as if God cares how we live. Given that we cannot definitively determine God's existence or nonexistence, nor discern the nature of God through objective, scientific means, what is the wise choice in light of the uncertainties?

Pascal presupposed that God rewards belief and righteousness with eternal bliss, and punishes disbelief and sinfulness with unending anguish. The philosopher posited that, under these circumstances, we should "bet" on God and believe/live a righteous life. If we do, the rewards will be infinite for us if God exists, while our losses will be insignificant if there is no God. If God exists and we reject God, we have lost everything; but if there is no God and we have believed in a fiction, at least we have led a good life and have not truly lost anything. From a risk/reward, cost/benefit standpoint, Pascal's analytical method favors decisions that err on caution's side when the stakes are high...the "better safe than sorry" school of thought.

Pascal's Wager can be applied in contexts very different from the religious/moral dilemma for which he formulated it. It is an action-oriented tool of great power and flexibility. Pascal identified a key issue all leaders must face, a formidable information-gap puzzle: How do we know what we do not know, and how does that uncertainty affect our decisions on important matters?

In other words, when crucial decisions depend on the answers to one or more questions for which we can't obtain a definitive answer, what is the best course of action? It is tremendously important that we look the correct way at the missing links in our information chain. Otherwise, we make the dreadful mistake of assuming that all those question marks surrounding many of our challenges add up to mean we should take no action. That's the mistake the Cubs have made when they've prematurely counted their pennants as won: They've forgotten that such uncertainties are why they actually play the games.

A Cubs Fan leader can use Pascal's Wager in the following way. First, determine whatever variables exist that are relevant to making a major decision. Then, decide what the largest and smallest results might be, both good and bad, from taking any of the divergent courses of action available.

Next, decide approximately (or, to continue with this book's baseball theme, come up with a ballpark estimate of) how probable or improbable each extreme outcome might be; that is, how likely is it that either the very best or very worst results will actually happen.

Finally, compare the magnitude of the consequences. Do this for each of the main variables, considering each possible combination of potential extreme values, in light of the probability that they will occur. It should be clear from the results where the greatest risks and rewards lie based on the menu of options at the leader's disposal.

Let's bring Pascal's Wager close to home (maybe a bit too close for comfort for some of us) with a real-life example from the personal experience of the humble, devoted authors of this book. Maybe you can relate. Every year, as our respective birthdays approach, our doctors send each of us a reminder that we're due for our annual physical check-up. Part of this recurring ritual features a dialogue with ourselves that consists of an internal debate over whether it's worth it. This little silent argument nicely follows Pascal's analytical framework on a personal, individual level.

There are some knowns and unknowns involved in our problem of whether to get our yearly physical. Among the knowns are the following minus factors: It will take about two hours' worth of time from our schedule to go to the doctor's office; it will cost us a small amount of money; and we don't enjoy the exam itself (particularly the parts consisting of the doctor's rubber-glove-covered fingers and one of our orifices). There are also some unknowns, both plus and minus: The exact amount of time the exam will require; precisely how uncomfortable the process will be; how freezing-cold or just chilly-cold the doctor's hands will feel; and how annoying or pleasant we will find the time we spend in the office and in the examination room waiting for our turn. But there's one more unknown that is far more significant: Will the exam reveal a serious, even life-threatening medical condition? If it does, will the doctor discover our condition early enough to be able to initiate a course of treatment that could save our life and/or avoid a prolonged period of intense pain?

Pascal teaches us that we should weigh both the size and the likelihood of each factor before we make our decision. When we look at the situation in this light, it becomes clear that any minor inconvenience, expense, discomfort, and annoyance it will (almost certainly) cost us to undergo the physical exam, all of this is overwhelmingly dwarfed by the possibility that the exam could save us from a premature and agonizing death. Even if, as is thankfully the case, it is relatively unlikely that any given exam will reveal a dreadful hidden medical problem waiting to kill us, the sheer incalculable magnitude of the benefits we'd receive from this early intervention makes it a wise choice to have the physical. A small chance that the exam will spare us a horrible and early death is good enough for us.

Even a low probability that an annual physical will give us another 20 or 30 good, healthy years to enjoy with our loved ones and fend off unbearable pain and suffering is sufficient—under the helpful lens given to us by Pascal—to outweigh any combination of comparatively insignificant countervailing factors on the other side of the equation. Don't you agree? After thinking about our options in these terms, we take a deep breath and tell ourselves, "Better safe than sorry," and make the darn appointment, often without even realizing that we have good old Blaise Pascal to thank for our good sense.

In this way, Pascal's Wager allows us to conceptualize the benefits and risks inherent in any determination so we can appreciate whether certain "bets" are wise or foolish. In essence, Pascal's Wager is a guide to rational gambling where the stakes are extraordinarily high, and where the decision-makers must find a reasonable way of dealing with huge unknown factors. The leader can consider the likely outcomes from each combination of extreme values for each variable in comparison with one another to evaluate whether there is a greater risk from non-action or a greater reward, and vice versa.

In a large percentage of scenarios, leaders have two main options, and one or more unbridgeable gaps in our knowledge of crucial facts. The consequences for guessing wrong and making the wrong wager are often far more momentous on one side than on the other. Leaders frequently find that the set of options in a given decision is analogous to those weighed in Pascal's Wager.

We have basically two choices—to devote significant time, money, and effort toward preventing a possible type of loss or not. There are usually important unknowns relevant to the issue of which option is preferable. The unknowns cannot be known, at least not without a finely-tuned crystal ball. But we do know that a decision to take preventive measures against a catastrophic loss has the possibility of paying immense, nearly infinite dividends, with only relatively minor negative consequences under the worst case scenario.

We also know that a decision to count our pennants before they're won, and not to prepare for a reversal of fortune, could lead to horrific, nearly infinite harm to our organization; but it could only offer comparatively small rewards (in terms of resources saved) even under the best of circumstances.

In this type of situation, the rational decision would be to plan for the best but prepare for the worst, until the goal is actually achieved. This option nearly eliminates the possibility of ruin while opening the door to limitless gain.

Of course, there is usually a wide range of possible actual values for each unknown, on a constantly-evolving continuum stretching from very high to very low. But leaders can simplify their use of Pascal's Wager by choosing only the extreme end-point values for ease of understanding. When there is a reasonable chance that a terrible outcome might be averted through advance countermeasures, the process often yields the outcome that a reasonable amount of precautionary preparation is appropriate.

If we invest a meaningful but not exorbitant amount of money and effort in preparing for a devastating loss (through additional training, practice, analysis, strategic planning, etc.), the only downside—if it turns out such measures weren't actually needed—is the "waste" of resources that might have been spent (or saved) for other projects. It is properly considered "unused insurance," conceptually no more a waste or a foolish investment than any of the (one would hope many) payments we make on our life insurance premiums during all the happy years we continue to remain alive.

Personally, we are rather pleased as every year passes without the need for anyone to file a claim under our life-insurance policies. *That means we're not dead yet!* We do not view the premiums we paid on the policies during that year to be a waste of money that could have been better spent on a high-definition television. We don't exclaim, "What a fool I was to squander my hard-earned money on that stupid life insurance stuff! I'm canceling my policy right now!" If we did ever blurt out anything along those lines, you can rest assured that we would never live to cancel our policies, and the insurance company would soon be writing a check to our wives or husbands—we mean widows or widowers.

On the other hand, there is an unimaginable cost from failing to take prudent countermeasures if it turns out that they were needed. If we sit on the sidelines and fail to invest in life insurance, and we "get lucky" (no disaster this time around), our only gain is in the form of saving the money and effort we could have spent on the preventive measures. Even if this amounts to sizable amounts of money, time, and effort in a given a year, it is a small benefit compared to the incalculably catastrophic losses we could suffer if we guess wrong in betting on the inaction option. When we count our pennants before they're won, we had better be sure we're counting real wins, not mirages.

Pascal's Wager can actually under-represent the extent to which the rational decision is to invest in failure preservation. Because the Wager appears to devote equal weight to each of the possible combinations of extreme polar variable values, it can mislead leaders into thinking that each of the outcomes is equally probable. This is most emphatically not the case, because some of these results are far more probable than others. As the Cubs have often proved, anything that can go wrong will, and bad things happen to good people.

This problem of apparent equality of disparate results is of the same type as a chart that depicts a person's chances, on any given day, of being fatally injured on the way home from work by a plummeting comet. There are only two possible results in such a table (survives another day, or squished by comet), and they would occupy an equal amount of tabular space on the printed page. But the probability of the former outcome is, thankfully, much higher than the likelihood of the latter tragic event. It's a vital facet of a leader's responsibility to assess, accurately, which theoretically possible events (both favorable and unfavorable) have a probability sufficiently high—in light of the results associated with them— that they should be factored into the decision-making equation.

By understanding and using logical tools such as Pascal's Wager, a leader is better prepared to make the correct decisions regarding what precautions to take. No one needs to go so far in avoiding the premature-pennant syndrome that they become paranoid pessimists. But a leader who intelligently identifies and weighs the relevant variables can make adjustments along the way, and will be more apt to achieve actual victories, not just bitter disappointment.

2nd Inning Discussion Questions

1. What accounts for the tendency in some people to become complacent and to take for granted a successful outcome prematurely?

2. How can a leader keep the organization centered and focused on doing what it takes to excel every day, over the long haul?

3. How would you compare the relative risks of a team becoming complacent and overconfident when doing well versus giving in to hopelessness and defeatism when doing poorly? What should a leader do to counteract either form of dysfunctional reaction?

4. What would your principal rival say is your greatest weakness in the area of creative planning?

5. Behind your back, what do you think your workers say about your long-term strategic planning skills?

6. What do you think about the College of Coaches idea?

7. What would happen if some variation of the College of Coaches system were implemented in your organization? Have you already experienced it? With what results?

8. Have you ever known of a leader who did more harm than good? If so, would a "leaderless leadership" structure, perhaps along the lines of the College of Coaches, have been an improvement?

9. What are the strengths and weaknesses of a rotating system of leaders, compared to the traditional one-leader approach?

10. What would be the results if your organization eliminated your leadership position and replaced it with a frequently rotating system of temporary leaders, drawn from a pool of experienced employees?

11. What is your opinion of Pascal's Wager as a decision-making aid? What are its strengths and weaknesses, as applied to your biggest leadership dilemmas?

12. How should a leader plan for very low probability but very high damage contingencies? When is it correct to ignore them?

13. What are the consequences of guessing wrong in either discounting or overvaluing a specific improbable but high-impact threat to your own organization?

3rd Inning
Farm for the Future

There are many theories as to why the Cubs have gone a century of seasons without tasting world-championship champagne. But one theme recurs: Their organization has habitually failed to do what it takes to locate, attract, train, and develop young talent with any degree of consistency.

A "farm system" of minor-league teams should rejuvenate and improve the major-league team with a dependable supply of good, fundamentally sound, and highly skilled young players. But this often has been missing in action for the Cubs. Teams such as the Los Angeles Dodgers and the Atlanta Braves have thrived year after year by bottom-to-top emphasis on instilling a winning attitude, mastering the basics, learning the fine points of winning, and developing every player's potential. Meanwhile, the Cubs have usually been forced to depend on trades and free-agent signings to shore up a sporadic internal supply of top talent.

A good farm system creates synergy. When significant numbers of novices rise step by step through the organization together, they develop friendships and a sense of common mission with one another. Similar to the military-boot-camp experience, team members who learn, struggle, live, work, play, travel, chat, spend idle hours together, and grow alongside one another gradually forge bonds through that shared experience. That collective formative set of experiences, given sufficient time, will foster mutual loyalty, teamwork, personal chemistry, group identity, security, trust, support, cooperation, know-how, and camaraderie. Each person knows more about every teammate's abilities, weaknesses, attitudes, and motivations, and learns to complement them as part of an organic unit. For teammates who "grow up" side by side, something of value can spring from every interaction, even such prosaic no-action activities like waiting for a bus or sitting in a hotel lobby. Something is always happening under the surface when people are together, even when it seems nothing at all is going on.

There is no adequate substitute for the root-forming advantages that emerge from extensive mutual experience "down on the farm." The deep-rooted network of unifying forces we're talking about takes months and often even years to initiate, grow, thrive, strengthen, and mature. Some of it happens by design, and some naturally on its own, just from people doing lots of things together for a long time. It simply cannot be quick-fixed by suddenly grafting a bunch of new arrivals from various other organizations onto a preexisting group. A large, cohesive "band of brothers" core must form at the team's center if it is to perform like more than a disjointed gaggle of individual strangers who merely clutch paychecks signed by the same person. Roots don't know any shortcuts.

It takes a patient, visionary leader to assemble a group of talented but inexperienced people, and then keep them together in a positive environment long enough for these subtle benefits to emerge. In any highly competitive context, pressure always mounts: Excel in the short term! Win now!

Upper-level leaders sometimes are unwilling to wait for new performers to mature as a unit. For anyone who isn't physically present "on the farm" where the next generation of stars is developing, at any given snapshot of time it easily can look like not enough is happening. This instant-gratification mindset can create intense pressure on leaders to short-circuit the farming process, prematurely weed out slow developers, rush the most promising prospects before they're ready, and not wait all those months and years. An impatient leader under such competitive constraints finds it virtually impossible to wait faithfully while roots may or may not be growing, unseen, beneath the surface. It is much quicker, easier, and more obviously active to pluck a few of the most obvious talents from the crop early, then head to the market to fill the basket.

But a caring leader, who understands both the importance and the nature of farming, will fight hard for the extra time the new performers need. He or she knows this: It's vital that those young talents learn all the skills and attitudes necessary for success, and spend significant amounts of time *together,* as a group. Leaders forge teams by allowing a critical mass of mainstays ample opportunity to work and play, win and lose, learn and live, concentrate and relax, sweat and loaf…right there alongside one another.

Wise leaders know they can't rush this any more than a farmer can make a field of corn ripen faster by harvesting it a month before it's ready. The ineffable bonds of friendship and team identity are more like slow-roasted peanuts than microwave popcorn. It requires a strong, over-the-horizon leader to remain calm during all the "wasted" time when it looks like nothing useful is happening. Often the deepest roots and the most enduring supports of a team develop in hiding, unseen, during lengthy periods of shared experience; even—or especially—during unplanned, unregimented, off-the-clock time together with peers.

The dictionary is the only place where success comes before work. The Cubs have often sought the easy way—and the easy way has led to hard results. Good leaders understand the truth behind the familiar alliterative slogan: Preparation prevents poor performance.

Failure to develop a long-term farm system as a means of ensuring a reliable supply of the right players at the right time has proven a critical Cub failure. While their competitors were able to count on a relatively steady infusion of bright new standouts developed from within, the Cubs have usually had to try on an ad hoc basis to plug big gaps in their own home-grown teams.

Sometimes they didn't hire the right talent scouts, or use their scouts effectively to scour the bushes for raw prospects. The way they inculcated sound fundamentals and a winning attitude in their newest players in the minor leagues was also less rigorous and less thorough than the training programs used by their more successful rivals. Moreover, because the stream of talent was undependable and meager, few young Cubs who made it to the major-league team had already formed strong bonds with one another—the type only created through years of close interaction during the developmental phase. Cubs rookies thus were often less talented, less skilled, less bonded to one another, and less disciplined than those bursting onto the scene for other organizations.

To try to make up the shortfall left by these inadequate recruits, the Cubs have resorted to hiring older, more seasoned players away from other teams. These proven performers, of course, don't come cheaply. They are in great demand, and often several teams are willing to throw piles of money at them to win the bidding war. They command top dollar, To try to make up the shortfall left by these inadequate recruits, the Cubs have resorted to hiring older, more seasoned players away from other teams. These proven performers, of course, don't come cheaply. They are in great demand, and often several teams are willing to throw piles of money at them to win the bidding war. They command top dollar, much more than the typical young rookie during those first several years. So the team must spend a disproportionately large fraction of its budget on each migrant star, with all the risks inherent in such a concentration of investment. Expensive mid-career, lateral hires have sometimes performed well (*see* Sammy Sosa, Andre Dawson, Moises Alou, Derrek Lee, Alfonso Soriano, and others), but then that's why the Cubs were willing to pay them such exorbitant salaries.

What really hurts is when a huge expenditure ends up in a heap of injury, bad attitude, and/or low productivity, as in the case of such major disappointments as George Bell, Danny Jackson, Todd Hundley, Nomar Garciaparra, and myriad others. But that's the gamble the Cubs took when they didn't pay enough attention to growing their own. As the saying goes: *You can pay now or you can pay later; but you will pay.*

As with many components of winning leadership, there is nothing glamorous, thrilling, or attention-snatching about this "law of the harvest" groundwork. It's nothing but indispensable. Too many leaders and managers seem convinced that training, mentoring, and professional development for themselves and their people is a waste of time and money. Because the payoffs are deferred until an indeterminate future date, and are imperceptible—even invisible—in the short run, these bottom-line nose-to-the-grindstone types see only needless expense and pointless effort in the costs to educate and prepare their team members.

No question about it: Equipping players with the best skills and inculcating young people with the right attitude require a substantial investment of funds, person-hours, and focused work. This amounts to a lot of money, moments, and motions that the organization could devote to its actual present-day business, to just "get it done." We may appear to neglect our actual work when we take time out to engage in training and education, which can look a lot like just sitting around. But Abe Lincoln had the issue properly framed when he said, "If I had nine hours to chop down a tree, I'd spend six hours sharpening my axe."

To run a farm system, or any type of farm, takes patience and acceptance of deferred or even denied gratification, plus full readiness to deal with the hard fact of no guaranteed payoff. The brightest prospects can fizzle out like dud fireworks, and the ones who do make it may not stay for very long. Let's look at that latter possibility for a few minutes, because myopic leaders tend to use it as an excuse to cut corners on talent development.

Prior to the 1970s, baseball players were contractually bound to remain with the team that signed them, year after year, almost like modern-day serfs. The so-called "reserve clause" in every player's contract gave the team's leadership the unilateral power to decide whether each player would stay with the team for the following season. Irrespective of who they were and how well they performed, players had only two choices: perform for their current team, or quit baseball entirely. Such a feudal system gave every team the opportunity to derive absolute maximum return on investment from its farm system, because it was solely within the team's discretion whether the home-grown players stayed or left.

But now, in the post-reserve-clause era, carefully cultivated stars can leave their original team as free agents after a few years. This new freedom is very frustrating to management, who now must compete with all other teams to retain the services of every player, including the prized stars they invested so much to develop initially. They see the situation as if their own children were jumping ship from the family business to take a better offer and join their arch-competitor. "After all I've done for you, this is the thanks I get...."

Modern-day workers in many other fields often migrate too, much more than they did a few decades ago. There is a perceived lack of loyalty or long-term commitment by both player/worker and management who long for the mythical good old days. But even though the harvest is not guaranteed to last for long, or to come at all, it is still by far the correct strategic option to farm for the future.

You cannot sustain a team solely by picking off the fruit of others' groundwork. It is too costly, too unpredictable, and too dependent on uncontrollable outside factors. We need to sow the variety of seeds we've chosen for ourselves, and care for them the way we think best. Many seeds will not germinate, and many young sprouts will not thrive, while still others may bear fruit for someone else; but our success depends on investing in the seeds that could one day become productive for us.

The farm system in baseball, and farming in general, is a very rich metaphor for a vital facet of leadership. If you are impulsive, impatient, immature, or im-anything, farming is not your ideal career. The rewards for a farmer's job well done are uncertain, unfairly at the mercy of external forces, and slow to develop. For a very long time, there may be no obvious evidence that anything good at all is being produced by all those weeks and months of difficult, protracted labor coupled with a sizable investment of money, supplies, physical requirements, and personal attention. A wheat farmer endures all that, and must be ready to begin all over again if a hailstorm, drought, insect infestation, fire, flood, or other treacherous turn of ill fortune sweeps everything away.

No one promises the farmer so much as a single loaf of bread from all that expense and exertion. Similarly, the leader of a baseball team has to be willing to pour large amounts of money, time, and talent into building and refining a productive farm system capable of bringing a fairly dependable supply of solid young players to the big club every year or so.

Akin to a good farm system in baseball, any other type of organization also uses a formal process to identify next-generation leaders and top workers early in their careers. These future key performers' career paths are planned strategically to build an array of required skills, cultivating young workers for important roles. These paths range from prolonged work assignments to short-term projects, as well as formal courses and in-place training. The journey is designed to teach leadership and functional skills, company values, and an organizational culture based on purpose, integrity, and ethics.

Leaders with any type of farm system (read that to mean *all* leaders) must accept this fact: Many of the promising recruits they work hard to identify, attract, and train will never advance to the next higher level of development, let alone become a major contributor at the highest organizational level. A lot of seed never sprouts, or isn't properly nourished, or is blown away on the wind, or is gobbled up by someone else. That's part of farming—an inevitable, unavoidable price to pay for any chance to reap an eventual bumper crop.

Farming isn't what it used to be, and neither is job-related training. Old-school types who ignore the changes are sowing the seeds of their own defeat. The tried (and trite) and true old tricks often don't work on the new dogs in this year's workplace.

That's at the center of what leaders really do—and really need to do—to succeed now. People entering today's workforce differ from the entry-level employees of even a couple of decades ago, which presents a leader with a jumbled grab-bag of adversities and advantages. They may have shorter attention spans, less acquaintance with strict standards, and diminished experience with long, arduous tasks. Today's young workers—even those with college diplomas and advanced degrees—may lack some basic skills and background knowledge once taken for granted.

As our educational system has been transformed—with much less emphasis on fact learning, rote memorization, and the fundamentals of reading, writing, mathematics, spelling, grammar, logic, and other disciplines—our graduates require much more remedial education and training before they can perform at an acceptable level in many jobs...and the leader has to provide that education.

Even graduates from elite universities and law schools can be surprisingly deficient in some of the skills needed to do actual work. They are not ready, off the shelf, to perform without a significant infusion of practical training on the job. Although exceptionally bright, they have never been asked to master the mundane but essential competencies that teachers not long ago drummed into ordinary students in public elementary schools. Also, the degree of awareness of major milestones of history, science, and culture among young graduates is very different (that is, much lower) from the norm of the previous generation. A leader cannot rely on an acceptable level of any of them until he or she has carefully assessed each person's readiness.

On the other hand, the young graduates now are far more technologically sophisticated than the previous generation of new employees. They usually can teach their leaders a thing or sixty about computer-aided research, software, hardware, personal digital assistants, and a host of powerful modern tools. They can handle all manner of telecommunication and high-speed computerized methods with a facility that will astound many old-timers who climb on a chair if someone mentions a mouse in the office. The wise leader is humble enough to use this digital edge to the fullest, even while filling in the young associates on some basic writing and socio-cultural fundamentals.

The farmer-teacher-leader cannot safely assume anything about new workers in terms of knowledge, skill, or attitude...only that they are human, and will surprise in ways that range from delightful to dreadful. If entry-level employees (or even senior ones) appear to have a work-ethic deficit, or seem disrespectful or ill-mannered, no contemporary Attila can change all that by merely barking a few orders. People have a deep-seated and ineradicable need to achieve and succeed. But a modern leader must find the right way to access that latent potential within each individual; and this often entails considerable teaching and back-to-basics skill training in the workplace. Screams, threats, and periodic exclamations of "You're fired" or "You just don't fit in" will not compensate for decades of acculturation and educational priorities that are a bit (or a lot) off track from what the leader wants from his or her people.

Teaching and learning are both central to what today's leaders really do; and that continues throughout the lifecycle of their relationship with their workers, which is why we will later touch on the concept of perpetual learning. Ignore either teaching or learning for long, and someone new soon will be in the leader's office that better "fits in" the 21st Century boss's chair.

The Cubs' management has so often failed to grasp this truth: The first duty of a leader is to grow more leaders. Too infrequently, the Cubs have signed or developed great young players without needing to resort to cherry-picking them from some other major league team. A golden handful or two of home-honed standouts—such as Ernie Banks, Ron Santo, Billy Williams, Greg Maddux, Mark Grace, and Carlos Zambrano—sprinkled on Wrigleyville teams through all these decades, stands out all the more within the Cubs' system precisely because they are rare exceptions to the team's usual pattern. But internally developed excellence in skill, talent, and leadership simply can't be a rarity in any team that hopes to win.

Now more than ever, leaders must teach, and teach deeper into the organization. This is essential if the leader is to be a force multiplier, and if the talent on his or her team is to take root and proliferate. This nurturing process has benefits for everyone involved, because when you teach, you learn twice, and twice as much as your pupils.

Thus, the best leaders are first and foremost a hybrid between teachers and farmers. They bring to the team a surplus of patience, optimism, insight, knowledge, skill, and willingness to work hard 24/7/365. They understand that bountiful harvests don't grow on their own, and don't happen by accident. This is a basic lesson that was lost on dozens of Cubs teams that tried to get by without paying the price in either effort or expenditure.

Many people lack the attributes necessary to be a farmer. They prefer to shop at the supermarket. It's quick, air-conditioned, easy, doesn't get you dirty, causes no unsightly calluses, and requires little more than money. But people are a different type of "commodity," and you can only lure the ones who are willing to be lured, and who have been schooled according to another team's core values. As a shopper, you can eliminate all that lengthy, arduous, slow, patience-stretching groundwork; but only at a price—much costlier team members with talents honed by a foreign formula. No matter how much you pay, you can only buy what someone else has prepared for you. But farmers can shape the harvest they reap by selectively planting the desired type of seeds; choosing which early sprouts to weed out; opting for whatever varieties of fertilizer, pesticides, and supplements they prefer, and gauging when the crop is ready to gather in.

We can conceptualize this farmer/shopper dichotomy using a simple mathematical formula for a quantity we will call the Quotient of Impatience (Q.I.). Don't be afraid. If you're any kind of Cubs fan, you've survived a lot worse than a little bit of math. This formula isn't intended to be mathematically rigorous, but rather just a helpful tool: a conceptual framework for a leader to balance the key variables relevant to any good farm system.

A leader who is aware of Q.I. as a basic analytical concept should be better able to conduct productive internal assessments, and make the changes needed to optimize his or her talent-development network.

$$Q.I. = [(V-C) \times Pr] / Pt$$

Where

V = Value of the harvest
C = Cost of planting/cultivating
Pr = Probability of reaping the harvest
Pt = Probable waiting time from inception to harvest

Q.I. increases as the expected value of any eventual result rises (V), and/or the transaction costs of the farmer's groundwork fall (C), and/or the likelihood of attaining a large harvest climbs (Pr)—all as expressed in the numerator—combined with a decrease in the lag time duration from the outset of the farming process through harvest season (Pt).

A large Q.I., with its quick payoff, demands relatively less patience from a leader. But a smaller Q.I. is slower to pay dividends, and thus more likely to spur overeager present-tense gratification seekers to conclude that the entire project isn't worth the costs and delays. When the Q.I. is comparatively greater, even an impatient leader is more apt to conclude that the cost/benefit expected value justifies the acceptably moderate lead time necessary to achieve that outcome.

Sadly, the Cubs management at all levels has often suffered from a low Q.I. (and perhaps a low I.Q. as well), and they have not suffered alone. The whole organization and all their fans have been forced to live with the devastating consequences of premature and hasty decision-making. Their chronic impatience has caused them to give up on some of the greatest budding stars of all time, only to see their castoffs bloom and come back to punish them for many years afterward. We will look in detail at two prime examples, Lou Brock and Greg Maddux, a bit later in this book. But there are numerous other instances in which managerial Q.I. deficiencies derailed the Cubs' train just as it was preparing to pull out of the station for a successful journey.

The point of Q.I. isn't to revive long-suppressed bad memories of math-class anxiety. On the contrary, Q.I. is a tool we've created to illustrate some leadership opportunities, or ways in which a savvy leader can identify aspects of a difficult situation that may be partially within his or her control.

Once a leader is aware of the main pertinent factors, and the manner in which they are interrelated and interdependent, he or she can do something productive about it. Conceptual formulas such as Q.I. are a device to assist leaders in gauging the situation at hand, and constructing a workable plan to exert positive influence in those areas amenable to modification and tactical reconfiguration. Such a formula can show us the difference between factors beyond our control and elements we might reasonably expect to mold to our team's advantage. So put your old math aversion on hold and take a look at this Q.I. equation with a fresh perspective, and an eye toward using its framework to improve your capacity to farm for the future.

The variables that comprise Q.I. can be influenced to some extent by the way in which a leader handles the farm system. A team of expert talent assessors, successful teachers and mentors, and a strong core of supportive workers at all levels can help a farm system function more quickly and efficiently, with better results, and at less cost. For example, if you can detect the early foreshadowing of budding talent before anyone else notices it, you naturally should be able to bring it on board for less money than if you are just one of many bidders for a known rising star.

Only a keen-eyed, seasoned, well-schooled observer can spot these subtle hints; but there are great rewards available to leaders who can foster such a skill set. And if you can create and maintain an effective, coordinated mechanism for systematically developing and training the young performers you do acquire, you should be able to bring them up to highly productive levels of maturity more quickly than less-capable farm systems, and with a greater success rate.

An integrated development program run by competent professionals can shift one or more of the Q.I. variables—such as cost, potential value-added payoff, likelihood of a successful result, and duration of lag time—in a favorable direction. The components of Q.I. should be considered in this light: not as fixed and immutable constants, but rather as variables that will respond to the right leadership.

Not all leaders are rational in the way they analyze Q.I. Logically, a large Q.I., generated by some combination of a high probability of worthwhile ultimate output, coupled with a favorable output-minus-input remainder, should persuade a leader that it is prudent and appropriate to wait a considerable amount of time for this positive result to reach fruition.

But whether caused by external time and performance pressures or self-internalized immediacy and resource constraints, some leaders will nonetheless conclude that the delay is unacceptable. This is particularly likely when few if any objective indicia of progress are evident during the long interim gap between planting and harvest (or talent acquisition and attainment of productivity). That interval, if perceived as excessive, will drive down the Q.I. and move short-sighted leaders to short-circuit the farm system.

It takes an astute, experienced farmer to endure the natural germination and hidden-growth periods of apparent dormancy, wait out and adjust for the inevitable setbacks from pests or bad weather, and diligently continue to tend the crop in faithful expectation of eventual reward. If the farmer knows enough about how the process works, and is acutely attuned to subtle clues that progress is being made, he or she can navigate past even a relatively low Q.I., while less sophisticated or experienced people would prematurely abandon the project.

In truth, in the long run it actually costs much less and is far more efficient and rewarding (in both the practical and intangible sense) to develop our own talent from within our organization. Much better than to leave that difficult, slow, and expensive preparatory work to others, and then attempt to hire the ready-off-the-shelf veterans once they are fully equipped to be valuable contributors. Such capable, proven performers can command much higher salaries than inexperienced, entry-level people, and are in far greater demand, precisely because they are fully prepared to make a big, immediate impact on their team.

Thus, even if we can outbid all our rivals for their services, we will be forced to pay a premium price. Why not keep the Q.I. concept in mind and amortize the costs? We can just pay the price a little at a time (and pay it mostly to our own team members), while simultaneously fostering a sense of loyalty, common/shared experience, and cohesiveness within our organization. We sniff out promising prospects at the outset, and then invest in the people we already have. When we grow our own talent, we keep more continuity within our team, build strong internal relationships, retain the power to train our people exactly the way we want them trained, and ultimately spend less money for greater return on investment.

That's what good farm systems do in baseball; and that's why the concept is so relevant to other organizations as well. Proactive leaders on these successful teams invest what it takes to increase and deal appropriately with Q.I. They find and hire promising young players very early in their careers; painstakingly and consistently infuse them with sound fundamental skills; nurture pride in both the team and the larger organization, and dedicate themselves over the long term to ensuring a reliable, steady pipeline of home-grown talent at all levels. Farming for the future isn't flashy or fast, but it eventually wins championships, complete with the sparkly rings that champions wear. And it brings honor, respect, enduring bonds, and mutual admiration to the team and to all those who support it.

3rd Inning Discussion Questions

1. Are leaders in your organization demonstrating an acceptable approach to the Quotient of Impatience (Q.I.) in attracting and developing members of a productive team? How does their attitude affect people at all levels?

2. Which components of your organization's Q.I. are most readily changeable, in a positive sense? What could you do to make this productive change a reality for those factors in the Q.I. equation?

3. Which components of your organization's Q.I. are most resistant to positive change? What factors create and maintain this resistance? What might you do to transform some aspects of this challenge?

4. Can patience be learned, or is it an innate quality we are either born with or not?

5. How can leaders motivate people who believe training and development of new employees is a waste of time better spent "doing the job?"

6. What is your organization's equivalent of a baseball team's farm system? Is it effective in bringing well-trained new talent up through the various levels on a dependably regular basis? How does it compare to similar systems in other organizations?

7. If you had the power to make one, and only one, change in your organization's approach to developing young talent, what would you do?

8. If scientists from another planet came to observe your leadership methods, what would they conclude about the way you find, hire, and train new employees?

9. Do you believe we have the right people aspiring to be leaders, whether in politics, in business, or in the military? Are we educating and training them correctly? What forces influence this leadership selection and development process, for better or for worse?

10. What if any value comes from giving young, inexperienced professionals significant amounts of time together, including formal training, group travel, collaborative projects, and leisure opportunities? What benefits can flow from protracted collective experiences that are not available from isolated individual training or experience?

4th Inning
Panic Proves a Poor Strategic Tool

No one likes to be accused of wilting under pressure. Whether you call it choking, collapsing in the clutch, or failing when the chips are down, it amounts to the same thing—an inability to remain focused and effective when it matters most. Panic is a natural reaction to emergencies, but it is a decidedly suboptimal means for dealing with them. Of course, it is very difficult to "keep your head when all about you are losing theirs and blaming it on you," but, as Rudyard Kipling understood, that's what separates the adults from the kids, the champions from the also-rans, and everyone else from the Cubs.

This leadership axiom, like many others, is far easier to write about than to implement. It takes no special courage, maturity, wisdom, equanimity, or strength of character to exhort others to keep a cool head in the midst of chaos and imminent disaster. That's why armchair generals never earn medals and Monday morning quarterbacks never get drafted by professional football teams. But at least those of us fortunate enough to sit safely away from the bedlam can try to borrow some lessons learned at a very dear price by people who were less lucky.

This principle is a corollary of the idea that we should not take ultimate success for granted until we actually achieve it. The Cubs, on some of those ignominious occasions when they had seemed destined to win, only to collapse within sight of the finish line, exhibited the natural response many people have under such exigent circumstances. They panicked. Let's inflict some pain on ourselves and look at one particularly horrible recent example.

It happened during Game Six of the 2003 League Championship Series against the Florida Marlins. The Cubs began that series in top form, fresh from defeating the Atlanta Braves in the Division Series, and winning three of the first four games from the Marlins in the best-of-seven match-up. This meant the Cubs needed to win only one of the remaining three games to take it all and advance to the World Series. When they dropped Game Five it still appeared that victory was assured, given that the Cubs' two top starters were ready to go (Mark Prior and Kerry Wood, with a combined record that year of 32-17) and the series was moving back to Wrigley Field. But Chicago had lived with a losing legacy for many years, built piece by piece and hurt by hurt. So when the Cubs returned home, they were slapped in the face with a headline in the *Chicago Tribune* that taunted, "Nervous Yet?"

Despite such mass-media negativity, for a long time in Game Six everything was going precisely according to a happy-ending script. The Cubs held a 3-0 lead in the 8th inning and were five outs removed from their first World Series since 1945. Prior was pitching brilliantly, working on a three-hit shutout. Outside Wrigley Field, vendors had started to unwrap bundles of World Series merchandise to sell to tens of thousands of victory-starved Cubs fans. The celebratory champagne was already in the Cubs clubhouse, waiting to be drunk or dunked on delirious players. Although Juan Pierre reached base with a one-out double, Prior seemed to have the game and the pennant well in hand as Luis Castillo came up to bat.

The trouble began when an unfortunate young spectator named Steve Bartman (a Cubs fan, no less) thoughtlessly impeded Cubs leftfielder Moises Alou in his attempt to catch a pop fly in foul territory near the stands. The headphones-wearing Bartman did exactly what thousands of other spectators have done as a foul fly ball came down toward them—he tried to catch it. Replays (endless replays) failed to prove conclusively that Alou would have caught the ball even if Bartman had hit the concrete to give him a totally clear shot. But it didn't matter. All Hell broke loose, and of the many things you don't want to break loose, All Hell tops the list.

As the ball eluded him, Alou furiously slammed his glove down and screamed at Bartman. Mark Prior howled in rage as well, demanding umpire intervention. But the umpire refused to call Castillo out, finding no fan interference, and the Florida batter remained at the plate.

At that point it would have required nothing more than a mature exercise of self-control and poise for the Cubs to hold a brief conference on the pitching mound. They could have talked about it for a minute and given everyone a chance to calm down. Led by veteran manager Dusty Baker, they could have collectively resolved to put the incident out of mind and concentrate on getting the last five outs, one at a time.

After all, the batter had not even reached base. The Cubs still could get Castillo out, and press on as if it were just another foul ball. But none of these panic-prevention measures were in use within 1,000 miles of Wrigley Field that night. Instead, key players became furious, rattled, shaken, and fearful. Images of past collapses and stubborn curses stormed into the Cubs' minds, where moments before confidence and professionalism had resided. An entire season, filled with numerous triumphs and thrills, suddenly dissolved in panic and desperation. History was repeating itself, like a dog returning to its vomit.

Castillo ended up drawing a walk, with ball four being a wild pitch. Ivan Rodriguez singled in Florida's first run. Then young slugger Miguel Cabrera slapped what appeared to be an easy double-play ground ball directly at Cubs shortstop Alex Gonzalez. That routine double play would have ended the inning, and the Cubs still would have been on top 3-1 with just one inning to go. But under the incendiary circumstances, the normally reliable, sure-handed Gonzalez committed a devastating error, getting no outs rather than two on the play. Gonzalez's blown double play threw the Cubs into full shock-and-awe freefall. A Derrek Lee double suddenly tied the score and chased the trumped-ace Prior from the mound; but reliever Kyle Farnsworth couldn't settle down either. A couple of walks later, light-hitting Mike Mordecai smashed a bases-loaded double, and the Marlins didn't stop until they had amassed eight runs in the inning. The Cubs lost the game 8-3, their dreams in ruins.

Panic had ignited a conflagration of overreaction in which the whole season precipitously burned up. What could have been overcome as a minor delay en route to victory blew up into a catastrophe.

It wasn't because the incident itself was especially significant. Remember, "Bartman's Boner" was only a foul ball that wasn't caught—really just one more strike. Castillo was still just standing at the plate with a bat in his hands, and the Cubs still were ahead 3-0 with five outs to go and their ace on the mound. This wouldn't ordinarily seem to be a disaster. But it became a disaster because the Cubs' response to it proved so extreme. Screams of "fan interference," thrown gloves, eruptions of uncontrolled anger, refusal to take a deep breath and get back to business, plus a sudden loss of focus…it all happened so fast.

It was a classic leadership lesson brought to terrible life: It's not what happens to you, but the way you react to it. That's what is important, and that's what you have within your own control, no matter what. The Cubs' reaction created the crisis.

The Cubs immediately went from self-assured winners to nervous novices unable to field the most routine of double-play grounders or make the same high-quality pitches they had thrown all season long. All that experience melted like a dusting of October snow on an Indian summer day, because it never came under pressure of *this* magnitude. It all fell to pieces because of their panicked, reflexive, over-reaction to what should have been nothing worse than a foul strike.

The Cubs meekly lost Game Six, then returned the next day with their confidence shattered and their nerves in tatters. Still wriggling at Wrigley, the over-anxious Cubs dropped Game Seven behind their other ace pitcher, Kerry Wood. The Cubs suddenly were rattled, tense, demoralized, tentative, and fearful…and that combination doesn't win many trophies. Their pair of aces in the hole—their pocket rockets, their weapons of mass destruction, their bullets—were cracked by a bunch of no-name upstarts. With these back-to-back defeats of their two best pitchers, Prior and Wood, the Cubs lost a lot more than two baseball games. They lost a golden chance for a World Championship. Once again, there was to be no World Series for the Cubs.

But that's what panic can do. It is the solvent that makes great structures come unglued. Good leaders know this and take steps to avoid it. If we are not prepared to deal responsibly with a swift and unexpected downturn in our fortunes, we too are vulnerable to all manner of hasty, clumsy, unprofessional, and unwise decision-making.

Naturally, for some leaders there is much more at stake than the outcome of a baseball game, however crucial that game may be to legions of die-hard fans. In real life, leaders sometimes face genuine matters of life and death. In the military, in time of war, such is the stuff of daily encounters with a deadly threat. But leaders at many levels and in many fields of endeavor may also unexpectedly and without warning find themselves facing a crisis in which lives depend on the leader's ability to resist the instinctive panic mode.

Ever since September 11, 2001, every leader has had to acknowledge this unforgiving reality. In the age of terrorism, it would be foolhardy to assume that we are safe from more attacks, whatever our circumstances. And Hurricane Katrina has reminded us that nature also has the power to utterly wipe out our greatest cities. No matter where we live, where we work, and what our normal ambit of responsibility, we must do all we can to anticipate the unthinkable and prepare for the unimaginable. Unless leaders devote considerable resources to disaster preparedness—whether human-made or natural in origin—they will be likely to succumb to panic when normality is all at once displaced by apocalyptic horror.

There are several specific negative consequences that typically flow from panic. This cluster of calamities is extremely conducive to the situation usually described as "making the wheels come off." To help illustrate how panic suddenly loosens those proverbial wheels, let's briefly list some of the often-interrelated ways panic works its reverse alchemy. When we panic we tend to do most if not all of the following:

1. We try to do everything at once rather than methodically taking actions in proper step-by-step sequence.

2. We try too hard, and substitute force for skill.

3. We lose our sense of perspective, priorities, and balance.

4. We don't take time to think before trying a desperate reflexive action.

5. We forget to communicate, whether to share information or to receive it.

6. We get excessively nervous, angry, or frightened (or a combination of the three).

7. We try to recoup our losses immediately through reckless overreaction.

8. We neglect refreshing and sustaining supports such as rest, short breaks, nourishment, and sleep, even during lengthy crises.

9. We squander our remaining resources rather than conserving and rationing them methodically.

10. We focus on the negative and give in to wild fear.

11. We neglect to follow sound, basic, fundamental procedures.

12. We lose discipline and self-control.

13. We react based on raw emotion instead of rational reasoning.

14. We fail to take a little time to calm down or relax so we can respond appropriately to the initial flood of adrenaline.

15. We hastily assume the situation is much worse than it really is.

16. We fail to cooperate with others.

17. We rush to take swift action without considering our options.

18. We refuse to refer to or implement the plans available to us.

19. We don't pause, even briefly, to get organized or reorganized.

20. We insist on doing too much personally without effective division of labor and collaborative effort.

21. We surrender to impatience and the impulse to immediate reaction.

22. We rush every action to an unnaturally hurried extreme and make needless, careless mistakes.

23. We take irrational risks.

24. We succumb to pressure and subconsciously give up.

25. We lose our sense of humor.

26. We allow ourselves to get caught up in a stampede mentality in the midst of an atmosphere of general chaos.

27. We become overly cautious and tentative, abandoning our natural aggressiveness and willingness to take the initiative.

There are no facile solutions to the panic predilection, no inoculations we can undergo to render ourselves immune to a flustered, disproportionate, full-tilt, freak-out response when things suddenly go sideways on us.

The best we can do: Begin by becoming aware of the problem, and of the dangers inherent in panic. As follow-on to this, we can strive, methodically and vigilantly, to anticipate difficulties and take well-conceived countermeasures before they blossom into deadly disasters. We can plan ahead during more placid times to develop appropriate menus of options that we will then have ready at hand when the organic waste matter strikes the oscillating air-circulation device.

Few disasters are truly unforeseeable, although we might find them unthinkable. It is unpleasant and unsettling work to brainstorm prepared responses to terrible situations that might one day befall us; but this preparatory work is nowhere near as unpleasant and unsettling as having to cope with an abrupt and dire emergency on the fly. Just ask Mark Prior, Moises Alou, Alex Gonzalez, and Dusty Baker.

It does no good to exhort people not to panic. That's along the lines of telling someone "Don't lose" or "Don't think about Poppin' Fresh, the Pillsbury Doughboy." Not only is it entirely ineffective, but it can also generate the very reaction we most want to avoid. Panic is highly contagious; and once it begins to flare up, it tends to engulf everyone around. Prevention is the only cure, and it comes only from long, slow, judiciously designed, highly disciplined training and preparation. Under exigent circumstances, it is very natural for people to become afraid and flustered, and to forget to follow normal, commonsensical procedures. A fast-moving and perilous emergency is not conducive to calm, rational thought. But if leaders have properly trained themselves and their people, they have a much higher probability of doing the right things and averting a rout mentality.

This is a prime reason why frequent, regular, well-organized inculcation of the fundamentals ranks so high on any successful leader's list of priorities. The basic actions prerequisite to an organization's mission must be learned, and over-learned, until they become automatic. To accomplish this takes focused, repetitive drills faithfully replicated for so long that the underlying skills pass from routine to second nature.

Winning baseball teams do this every day, from their lower farm team up to the major league roster; and they do it during spring training on, before every game and on many days when there is no game. Perfect practice makes permanent; and if leaders carefully direct the practice toward the correct fundamentals, all that repetition will eventually plunge deep roots into the core of every member of the team. Only if this type of often-grueling, boring, drudgery groundwork is done and done and then done again will the leader have a team prepared to take correct action when everything suddenly depends on instinct, not deliberation.

There are learning moments, but they don't come on a strict, predictable timetable. We experience things over and over again, learning in a spiral, not a straight line. And then one day we get it. There is learning from repetition, but it only comes when all conditions are right and the people are ready.

A good leader will look for ways to make all this rehearsal less onerous and, where possible, fun. If no one is having fun, you are not doing it right. An infectious upbeat attitude can find methods that include games, contests, humor, and variety to help alleviate the numbing effects of repetitive practice. Training doesn't always have to resemble boot camp, as long as the central aim is always in sight. It pays to spend time and money searching for pleasant modes of training, because it will be a lot easier to motivate people to participate fully if they view the experience as something on the sunny side of unadulterated drudgery. This doesn't mean that a leader must always imitate a cheery counselor from a summer camp when structuring the training program, but it's okay to smile. It's okay to try to reduce boredom and make learning interesting. It doesn't make training less rigorous or less efficacious if people don't hate it. Medicine need not taste horrible to be powerful, and workers will be more cooperative if the experience can be sweetened a bit.

This can include injecting some variations into the repetitive theme—finding new avenues to inculcate the same skills by taking somewhat different routes at different times. Leaders encounter less resistance and more cooperation when they give their people training alternatives to the galley-slave paradigm. Leaders make it their mission in life to give a piece of themselves to everyone they encounter. The great coach Vince Lombardi reflected this in his mission statement: "Live a life of integrity and make a difference in the lives of others."

It will still require plenty of well-conceived repetition and reinforcement of correct principles over a protracted period of time, and under a wide range of conditions, if the leader is to minimize the risks of panic under fire. If this is to be effective, it won't always be easy, comfortable, and convenient. There's no substitute for hard work and regular, methodical review of fundamental precepts. Panic is a natural human response to unexpected and unfamiliar threats, and it is only by proactively anticipating those threats, analyzing what tools are needed to counter them, and providing a generous overabundance of sound, realistic training to create and reinforce those tools that leaders can shut off the panic reaction before it wreaks its awful damage.

Good leaders understand these panic prevention principles. They grasp the concept that organizations cannot grow unless people grow, including the leader and everyone else. We do not go to school once in a lifetime and then put education aside forever; we are in school all of our lives. Life itself is one great and unending learning opportunity, and our lives depend on taking full advantage of it—sometimes figuratively, and sometimes literally. This is especially true for the leader. But gaining knowledge alone—what once was called book learning—is not enough. If it were, the professors would rule the world...heaven help us!

On the contrary, it is people with knowledge who can also make knowledge work for those who move the world. They are the ones who survive even the direst of emergencies. In their role as teachers, leaders should make every effort to encourage their people to put into practice what they learn, because the true value of knowledge is being able to use it, especially under the most stressful conditions. Without marrow-deep practical competence, our personnel are dependent drones, helpless when the crunch comes. The future of our workforce will be increasingly competitive and fast-moving, both locally and globally.

Learning how to learn is the key to professional survival, and leaders must teach their people this core capability. When we do, we become more competent and crisis-ready ourselves. When we teach, we learn twice, and twice as much.

Sometimes, people resist the idea that they must continue to learn all their lives, particularly when the new material is strange, difficult, unfamiliar, complex, technologically advanced, and outside the normal zone of comfortable competence. They had unpleasant experiences in school, and associate learning with institutionalized boring, repetitive, stressful, mandatory drudgery.

But the modern life is a down escalator, and unless we are actively working to move up, we will be passively pulled downward by exterior forces, especially when a crisis hits. Every day there are changes, and some of those changes can affect our lives...positively, if we take advantage of them, and negatively, if we don't see new threats emerging. Awareness of this constant change requires regular study, openness to new information, and the flexibility to bend with the trends. It need not be boring. In fact, given how much is at stake, we should be wide awake to new information and recent digital-age advancements. That means reading widely and voraciously, and talking with people about things that matter to our work. It also means loosening our desk-bound shackles and putting our footprints all over the workplace and beyond, seeing for ourselves what's going on in that perilous and untidy spot known as the real world.

Some might assume that panic-prevention training and other forms of perpetual learning are largely a function of only a few inherently fast-evolving fields (such as information technology, medicine, science, and telecommunications) or obviously dangerous careers (such as the military, law enforcement, and firefighting). It may be that the state of the art moves at a more accelerated rate in some disciplines, but there is always advancement and adjustment in any human enterprise; and often innovations that began in one specialized context can be adapted to applications far removed from the field of origin. But it takes active creativity and a well-stocked knowledge base for people to be cognizant of these potentially useful breakthroughs in "foreign" disciplines, and to spy the possibility of cross-pollinating them into one's own quite different situation.

This is one primary benefit of leaders reading omnivorously and ravenously, and inspiring their people to do likewise—creating the capacity to make connections between seemingly disparate phenomena and turning the amalgam into something new and valuable. Hybridization of ideas, methods, tools, and technologies is a highly potent source of innovative improvement, but it most emphatically does not happen on its own, nor in adherence to some artificially imposed timetable. Cubs Fan leaders know they have to prime the pump, to scatter good seeds far and wide and often, and practice patience if it seems that "nothing" is being harvested from all this expensive and time-devouring exertion.

Perpetual learning in itself will not provide absolute panic immunity, nor solve all our other problems; but without continuous self-development, both formal and informal, we will not even realize what the problems are. It is critical for the leader to work hard to ask the right questions, which is the first step in determining everything else that requires the leader's attention, including key vulnerabilities. If we ask the wrong questions, or worse, ask no questions at all, none of the right answers will blow in through some air vent to make our dreams come true...or to make our nightmares vanish.

No organization accidentally grows ready to survive sudden disasters. A team becomes robust to unexpected dangers through the gradual, methodical process of perpetual learning. To achieve this, leaders need to think frequently, creatively, and fearlessly about what the organization's big questions should be. They ask their workers for their honest and frank opinions on what must be done, and then reward them for their input. The leader should keep in mind, too, that the biggest lie is this: We are as good right now as we are ever going to be—that this is as good as it gets. As if! In today's culture, true professionals understand that success is all about four-season growing, remaining flexible, and never ceasing to move toward the next level. Continuing education helps to get us there and become ready for the biggest challenges.

Naturally, as with most good ideas, many organizations have discovered a way to mess this up. As with mentoring, quality, and feedback, perpetual learning is susceptible to being loved to death. Large conglomerations of people tend to grab hold of such obviously worthy notions and (often with entirely good intentions) hug all the life out of them, like a giant python with a pet hamster. The fear is that nothing will get done, or what is done won't be done right, or no one will be able to tell how much has been accomplished and what still needs attention, unless the organization imposes/mandates plenty of structure, process, metrics, and substance.

The outcome, however, is often a system that has been routinized, measured, micro-managed, outsourced, mass-produced, formalized, over-preached, standardized, prepackaged, force-fed, and homogenized into yet another pro forma ritual dance of empty gestures. It begins with idealism, but gradually gets dragged into assembly-line pragmatism, and can even deteriorate into hollow cynicism. Professional continuing education in the workplace can so easily be transmogrified in this way, so that— in place of genuine individualized drill-down learning—we find a mandatory established church where the workers are the unwilling parishioners and migrant mercenaries are the soul-deficient clergy. Any real learning that comes from such canned and compulsory formalities happens virtually by accident.

Can Cubs Fan leaders save professional learning, particularly of the panic-prevention variety, from the march of the square-fillers? It's a daunting challenge, because many organizations have long had in place a deep-rooted über-forest of Continuing Education or Professional

Development, and don't forget to capitalize them. Everyone knows the dance steps. Everyone is accustomed to keeping careful records of which freeze-dried courses and conferences each worker has attended. Everyone knows the rite-of-passage certificates and mini-diplomas a person needs for his or her "I love me" wall in order to advance to the next stage of the game. Everyone is comfortable with the type of training where you literally mail it in. Plus, lots of folks gather lots of money from the pre-fab structure of frozen-dinner education, and they're not eager to give that up. Try even to modify this venerable ritual, this Cerebellum Ceremony, and the heavens may fall, let alone the cataclysm that could come from a push to discard it entirely. But a leader who assumes that this formalized, systematized cookie-cutter clone of perpetual learning is necessary and sufficient to serve all the workforce's authentic educational needs, including panic prevention, is a leader who is clutching a lifeline thrown to a mirage.

We can't rubber-stamp our way to the actual learning essential to staving off panic and staying competitive in the contemporary whirlwind environment. No stacks of parchment with boxes neatly checked off and squares fully filled in will compensate for employees who have not been taught what they truly need to know by dedicated and competent trainers with a continuing stake in how well the people actually perform. No false-front Hollywood set of a professional training system that mass-produces a pretentious line of faux courses can make up for failure to get our hands dirty on the difficult but indispensable job of teaching people one by one every day, by example and by increments, by sequential experience and by patient reminder.

Too often, true learning takes place—in spite of and not because of the officially sanctioned process—in an underground, samizdat network that operates in parallel with and quite apart from the orthodox educational artifice. Leaders might have to reserve their best teaching efforts for much-needed reality therapy as a supplement to the ritualized effects of an entrenched, make-believe, continuing-education bureaucracy.

Developing people—really developing them, with all the individually tailored effort that entails—is fundamental to how the organization views itself, and how it is viewed by leaders, customers, competitors, and colleagues alike. Perpetual learning is how the organization reifies its capabilities, by enhancing every person from the inside out, and working the same internal alchemy on the overarching team structure.

Only by holding the "Learning Constant" foremost in their vision can leaders have a chance of keeping their workers fully capable of fulfilling an ever-shifting mission under steadily unsteady circumstances. The complexity of life in the world today is such that there is no question that continuous learning and adaptation is directly related to, and absolutely essential for, overall long-term success. Life is learning and learning is life.

This type of rigorous and regularized training also helps to stave off panic by generating a healthy and justified self-confidence. Leaders must realize that the greatest power tool they carry is a trained and disciplined mind. People who are well prepared, and who know they are well prepared, naturally develop a steady sense of their own competence. They gradually acquire a deservedly high opinion of their capabilities, because they have seen the evidence of what they can accomplish accumulate over countless trial runs. When things go sour, they are less apt to choke in the clutch, because they have learned their own capacity to handle difficult situations; and they believe they can rely on the same resources that have brought them through those other challenges.

Leaders must make training not only realistic but tough, to give everyone experience handling a range of thorny problems. By preparing for the worst, leaders can help their people shrug off the inevitable hard luck situations and not come unglued when they encounter what Texas Hold 'em poker players call "bad beats." Bad luck, being in the wrong place at the wrong time, a freak occurrence—things like this can happen to anyone. But when they do, poorly equipped individuals are far more apt to "go on tilt," losing their composure, becoming angry and emotionally upset, abandoning their game plan, forgetting the need to be patient, and generally losing control. People who go on tilt greatly magnify the ill effects of any crisis. Conversely, people who train long and hard become inured to the many vagaries of fortune that eventually come to everyone. They are more able to maintain confident focus during bedlam-ready crises because they've been through it all before.

We can express these principles in a mathematical relationship we call the Coefficient of Panic Vulnerability (C.P.V.). This brief flirtation with mathematics isn't intended to induce panic in you, but instead to help you to avoid it, so please bear with us. It will be over soon.

$$C.P.V. = \frac{\{[(En \times S) - (Ep \times S)] + R\}^U}{T \times L}$$

Where

Ep = Collective positive/successful experience in past crises

En = Collective negative/unsuccessful experience in past crises

T = Amount of team's effective training in relevant fundamental skills

S = Degree of similarity between current emergency and prior experiences

L = Leadership's ability to rally the team in a crisis

R = Magnitude of the aggregate perceived risk/danger as viewed by the team

U = An exponent representing the extent to which the current crisis was unforeseen by leader and team

A *large* C.P.V. is *unfavorable*, signifying less ability to resist panic in a crisis. A *smaller* or fractional C.P.V. is *favorable*, representing greater immunity to panic in exigent circumstances. C.P.V., however, does not reflect a linear relationship of all its components. As the multiplier effect of T times L increases, the value of C.P.V. declines more aggressively once we move beyond a key inflection point. The synergy of T times L produces dramatic improvement in the team's resistance to panic once the inflection point is surpassed.

The good news is that we're not at the mercy of C.P.V. as if it were a force of nature entirely beyond our influence. We can, and we must, approach C.P.V. as a challenge that will respond favorably to our well-planned efforts. A Cubs Fan leader can exert a positive influence on his or her team's C.P.V. by orchestrating those variables that are at least partially within the leader's control. This requires substantial attention to the factors in the denominator, which are most amenable to the leader's transformational efforts, and which, as they expand, can produce a dramatic and desirable reduction in the overall C.P.V.

The leader can help craft and implement a well-conceived program of regular practical training (T) and refine certain facets of his or her own leadership traits (L) so as to augment crisis-preparedness. This purposeful elevation of T and/or L must actually be no-kidding effective to give a meaningful nudge on the team's C.P.V.

This is not in the familiar category of taking superficial steps to make things look better. The training, as modified, has to be intelligently structured so as to isolate and improve aspects of individual and collective knowledge, skill, attitude, and behavior that are in reality likely to make a difference under emergent conditions. Similarly, the leadership makeover should amount to more than just browsing through a few books (even this one); it will take dig-deep, get-your-hands-filthy hard work over a significant span of sustained effort to make changes that will really plus-up a leader's crisis-ready traits and boost the variable L.

In addition, the leader can reduce the crucial "unpleasant surprise" exponent (U) and head off the potentially disastrous and literally exponential multiplier effect it brings to a team's panic vulnerability. One does this by focusing the team's planning, training, and preparations on anticipating problems before they transpire. The greater the number and variety of potential crisis-sparking incidents the team can identify and construct countermeasures for in advance, the less vulnerable the team will be to panic if an actual emergency occurs.

This creative anticipatory initiative should involve a sustained effort by the whole group to conceive of a broad spectrum of possible vulnerabilities. This would entail forecasting of not only the general types of events that could threaten the team, but also a varied menu of specific means by which these threats could arise...not just the "what" but also the "how" of the potential emergencies. It is one thing to plan an occasional generic, pro forma fire drill, but quite another to train under pressured conditions for proper responses to fires in various locations, of various degrees, of various origins, and fueled by various combustibles (wood, oil, natural gas, electricity, jet fuel, gasoline, cooking grease, etc.).

A leader who assists her or his team to develop realistic virtual previews of potential urgencies across a wide expanse of methods, magnitudes, and means can contribute greatly in reducing the critical U exponent. As the leader prepares the team in this way, an increasing number of possible chaos-causers scoot from the dreaded unknown to the been-there-done-that comfort zone. This is where leadership has the opportunity to deliver the maximum value-added throw-weight, because of the exponential nature of the U variable.

The impact of U on a team's panic vulnerability is expressed as an exponent because of the central importance of the familiar versus unprecedented aspect in determining a stressor's shock effect. An urgent situation is tremendously more potent in its disorienting and unnerving blitz power when those confronted with it have never before lived through anything like it. But, as legions of combat veterans would attest, even the deadliest of wartime clashes can be manageable for people who have grown battle-hardened and accustomed to dealing with such terrors, and who are flanked by trusted, loyal allies with whom they've weathered tough challenges together. Troops on an experienced team, inured to battlefield pandemonium, maintain a lower order of risk to being routed under fire when compared to those fresh out of boot camp who have never known such bedlam. Hence, harnessing the exponential power of U warrants the very highest priority on a leader's disaster preparedness radar screen.

In building the team, a Cubs Fan leader can also reduce aggregate panic proclivity in this way: recruiting and retaining team members who have a considerable amount of successful experience in overcoming a variety of challenging exigencies. The addition of such crisis-capable veterans to the team can raise its overall positive experience base (Ep) and render it more accustomed to meeting and overcoming a wide variety of possible stressors. Conversely, if some individuals have had extremely negative and damaging, even traumatic experiences in struggling through past crises, and have been unable to deal with these effectively, a leader might as a last resort remove them from the team—an effort to reduce the group's collective unsuccessful experiential history (En). In this way, a leader can diminish the extent to which En exceeds Ep, and thus reduce the team's C.P.V.

Although En will almost always be greater than Ep in any collection of people—because of the very nature of emergencies as inherently dangerous, destructive, negative events—a leader has the power to shift that inequality downwards so that it approaches zero (an equal critical mass of favorable and unfavorable crisis experiences). As the preponderance of En over Ep is reduced, the team as a whole grows more robust to any future crisis and less prone to panic...and that is a vital part of any leader's mission.

4th Inning Discussion Questions

1. Would you say that your current organization has a favorable or unfavorable Coefficient of Panic Vulnerability (C.P.V.)?

2. Which of the elements of your organization's C.P.V. are farthest from optimal? Which are the most in line with the ideal?

3. Identify the components of your team's C.P.V. that are most amenable to positive change.

4. Which components of your team's C.P.V. would present the greatest challenge to a leader attempting to effect change for the better? Why?

5. What factors have shaped your organization's C.P.V. situation? How could your C.P.V. be optimized?

6. If your organization's approach to panic preparedness were a famous movie, which one would it be?

7. On a national scale, what assessment would you make of this country's collective C.P.V.? What does this mean for the nation during perilous times?

8. Is there truly anything a leader can do to insulate an organization from the panic reflex, or is panic prevention a futile endeavor?

9. When a group experiences a very painful, even tragic event, what can a leader do to help everyone grow and learn something positive from it?

10. To what extent might dwelling on past mistakes, in an effort to prevent recurrence, actually increase the likelihood that people will fall prey to the same pitfalls again? How should a leader guard against this tendency while still benefiting from "lessons learned" through prior misfortunes?

5th Inning
Don't Brock Yourself

Success at a world-class level requires keen insight on championship ingredients, and wisdom to recognize and keep key players whose ultimate value is still unclear. This applies to people, to ideas, to technology, and to a range of other components important to building and sustaining a great organization. If it were easy to identify diamonds in the rough when they still look more like chunks of rock, the Cubs would have been doing it all along; and they would have at least one or two world titles to show for their last ten decades of effort. Instead, the Cubs have given up on people too early, or overlooked the true potential of their young talent, or overestimated the value of other teams' already-proven stars—and often all of the above, all at once. They have repeatedly sold their birthright for a mess of messed-up has-beens, and missed out on the benefits of long and stellar careers subsequently enjoyed by their discards.

The most extreme example involves the trade of young outfielder Lou Brock. Of all the Cubs' outstanding bad leadership examples, this may be the king. So fasten your seatbelts; it's going to be a rough ride.

Lou Brock came up through the Cubs' minor-league system with a wonderful set of natural gifts, including a rare combination of speed and power; but like many inexperienced young players, he had difficulty living up to all the hype. By 1964, Cubs leadership had become disenchanted with their talented outfield prospect. A few days before Brock's 25th birthday, the Cubs agreed to a six-player deal.

Mainly, the Cubs wanted to unload Brock and his unfulfilled promise to the Cardinals for established veteran starting pitcher Ernie Broglio. The trade was actually a six-player deal with Lou Brock, Jack Spring, and Paul

Toth going to the Cardinals in exchange for Ernie Broglio, Bobby Shantz, and Doug Clemens. The Cubs thus received two big-name pitchers, because Broglio (then almost 29 years old) was accompanied by the 39-year-old Shantz, another former 20-game winner. While Shantz was clearly past his prime, Broglio still appeared ready to produce more big results. The deal seemed like a good idea to the Cubs at the time, given their skewed frame of reference. They swiftly went from skewed to skewered.

Broglio had led the National League in wins with 21 in 1960, and was just coming off another excellent year in 1963, having won 18. He was several years older than Brock and already a proven star, not just a bundle of theoretical potential. At the time of the trade, Brock had only shown flashes of raw talent, and he was struggling. He had compiled a lackluster batting average of just .258 with 24 stolen bases in 1963, and .251 with 10 steals before the trade in 1964. He had showed some signs of delivering on his speed/power promise, but only managed to hit nine homers in each of the prior two seasons—not bad for a lead-off man, but nothing eye-watering either. Cubs management decided it was time to give up on Brock as just one more ordinary player who failed to live up to great expectations. They reasoned: It isn't every day you can dump a mediocre youngster and get a certified star pitcher in return, with a couple of extra players thrown in on both sides of the deal.

The trade did not bring the results the Cubs had hoped for. During the remainder of 1964, Lou Brock performed like the Hall of Famer he is. After he left the Cubs, he batted a blistering .348 and stole 33 bases. He sparked his new team to the National League pennant and the World Series Championship over Mickey Mantle and the New York Yankees that same year. Meanwhile, the Cubs reaped a famine harvest from their new acquisitions. During what was left of the 1964 season, Broglio won just four games for the Cubs while losing seven. The following two years combined, he notched only three victories against 12 defeats, and then retired from baseball forever. No one else involved in the trade made any impact for either team.

It was bad enough for the Cubs to watch their longtime rivals, the Cardinals, immediately take the World Series behind Lou Brock in 1964. Couldn't they have waited at least a year? As every Cubs fan knows, though, that was only the beginning of the long, agonizing aftermath of the worst trade in baseball history. For the 11 seasons from 1964 through 1974, Brock proceeded to lead the league in stolen bases eight times, and finished second in steals the other three years. He capped this amazing performance by breaking the all-time records for stolen bases in a single season (118 in 1974) and in a career, breaking venerable marks once held by the great Ty Cobb in both cases. Twice he put together four-year streaks of winning the stolen-base title. Brock stood always at or near the top in runs scored as well, and he hit as many as 21 homers in a single season.

Most important of all, Lou Brock was the sparkplug for winning Cardinals teams year after year, including three trips to the World Series (in 1964, 1967, and 1968) and two World Championships (in 1964 and 1967). His composite batting average was a sizzling .391 in those three World Series, with 14 steals. You should already know how many times the Cubs made it to the World Series during those same years. In case you've forgotten, you can calculate the answer by taking the sum of Brock's stolen base totals from 1966, 1973, and 1974 (74, 70, and 118) and subtracting the result from 262.

Lou Brock's legendary speed and base-stealing ability were qualities conspicuously absent in the Cubs teams of that same era. Those Cubs teams that nearly won the pennant in 1969 and neighboring seasons suffered from imbalance due primarily to lack of base-running speed and any offensive weapon other than the long ball. A base stealer of even average stature, let alone a record breaker such as Brock, could have lifted the Cubs the short additional distance they needed to reach the top. After all, before he ended his Hall-of-Fame exploits, Lou Brock shattered both the record for most steals in a single season and in an entire career.

How the Cubs could have used him! What might have been if the powerful but slow Cubs teams that came so close to winning pennants in 1969 and 1973? Lou Brock easily could have been the sparkplug, the missing piece for those teams that needed exactly what he offered to go all the way.

By way of illustration, let's compare Brock's annual stolen base totals with the number of steals achieved by the Chicago Cubs' entire team during the seasons from 1965 through 1976. Remember, these charts show how one single player fared on the base paths as against another whole team, year by year.

SEASON	LOU BROCK'S STEALS	CHICAGO CUBS' STEALS
1965	63	65
1966	74	76
1967	52	63
1968	62	41
1969	53	30
1970	51	39
1971	64	44
1972	63	69
1973	70	65
1974	118	78
1975	56	67
1976	56	74
TOTAL:	**782**	**711**

This chart reveals some remarkable facts. During the entire 12-season period (the Dark Ages?) immediately following the Brock-for-Broglio imbroglio, Lou Brock *on his own* stole more bases than *everyone* on all those Cubs teams combined. Brock achieved his fast-feet feat in six separate individual seasons as well, including four years in a row. Moreover, it was usually a very close steals race even in those years when Brock didn't beat the whole Cubs team, whereas in certain seasons Lou stole far more bases than his entire former organization. He actually defeated the aggregate Cubs squad by a whopping 40 steals in 1974.

Yes, his speed might have come in handy for one or two of those near-great teams. And to make matters worse, Lou Brock was much more than just a sprinter. He was a fine, versatile ballplayer would could consistently hit for a high batting average, hit for power, field, rise to the occasion when it was most needed, and provide inspirational leadership for his team. The Cubs missed him for all of his phenomenal base-stealing prowess, and far more besides.

It was probably impossible for the Cubs to top Brock-for-Broglio as a stunning, archetypal example of leadership lazy eye. But the unbelievable fact is that they came very close. This is just one more reason why we have a book-load of lessons learned from the Cubs' mistakes. We're referring here to another "big one that got away": the superb starting pitcher Greg Maddux.

Maddux was a true rarity—an excellent pitcher actually developed by the Cubs within their minor league system. Greg made it to the majors with the Cubs in 1986, and by 1988 was one of the finest pitchers in all of baseball. He won 19 games for the Cubs' team that nearly captured the pennant in 1989, and then notched 20 victories for the first time in 1992. That year, Maddux was recognized for his pitching prowess with the Cy Young Award, the annual honor accorded to the top hurler in each league.

At that point, Maddux was still only 26 years old. He had firmly established himself as a consistent pitcher of the highest quality, free from serious injuries, and a fierce competitor. He was the type of starting pitcher a team's leaders always dream about when looking for someone around whom to build a winning organization. But then, we're talking about the Cubs, so you know this story must end tragically.

In the aftermath of Maddux's great 1992 season, contract negotiations broke down between him and the Cubs. The Cubs were unwilling to spend what it would take to retain the cornerstone of their pitching staff for the next decade or so. Ultimately, they let Maddux depart as a free agent, even though, unlike Brock at the time of his trade, Maddux had *already* established himself as a bright new star. He signed with the Atlanta Braves and, like Brock before him, immediately commenced to string together a collection of achievements that can only be described as indescribable.

During the 11 baseball seasons from 1993 through 2003, Greg Maddux never won fewer than 15 games each year. His new team, the Braves, made it to the postseason *every single one* of those seasons (except in 1994 when a labor strike forced cancellation of all postseason series). Astoundingly, he won the Cy Young Award three additional consecutive seasons from 1993 through 1995 (his first three years just after leaving the Cubs).

Ex-Cub Maddux led the National League with the best Earned Run Average four times during those next 11 years, and finished second best on three more occasions. This included seasons in which he allowed runs at such an astonishingly low rate that experts struggled to find any point of comparison since the twilight of the spitball and the dawn of the Babe Ruth slugging era in 1920. For example, during the high-offense years of 1994 and 1995, Greg's E.R.A.'s were a microscopic 1.56 and 1.63, respectively. In

1995, Maddux turned in a superhuman won-lost record of 19-2, and almost equaled that two years later when he went 19-4. His control was equally unbelievable. In several seasons he walked an average of only around one batter per nine innings, including such unheard-of averages as 0.99 in 1995 and 0.77 in 1997.

Quite literally, no one had ever seen anything like it. It was as if the immortal pitchers Christy Mathewson or his legendary Cub rival Mordecai "Three Finger" Brown had returned miraculously from their dead-ball epoch of long ago to repeat their masterful work in the midst of modern-day sluggers and juiced-up baseballs. Maddux's monumental achievements in combining near-perfect winning percentage, unimaginable E.R.A., and laser-sharp control pitching were all but impossible. Yet he did them all, and then did them again.

How were the Cubs faring while Maddux led his Braves to three World Series (including a World Championship in 1995) and postseason playoffs every possible time, that is, 10 consecutive years? In the unlikely event you are in the mood for another math riddle, here's how to figure out how many times the Cubs reached the World Series while Maddux's Braves were on this terrific roll. Add up Maddux's regular-season victory totals during the years from 1993 through 2003 (20, 16, 19, 15, 19, 18, 19, 19, 17, 16, and 16), then deduct his total number of losses in each of those years (10, 6, 2, 11, 4, 9, 9, 9, 11, 6, and 11). Finally, take that number and subtract 106. But then you already knew that, didn't you?

There are other cases, too, in which the Cubs prematurely gave up on a young, developing star in their pursuit of instant success and/or saving money. Rafael Palmeiro, Joe Carter, and Dennis Eckersley, among others, were discarded just as their careers were beginning to soar. Of course, no one can foretell the future with precise accuracy, but when talent of this caliber is under consideration, a bit of extra patience is in order.

This tendency to let future star performers slip away relates to the Cubs' deficient farm system. The same organizational mindset, paucity of judgment, and lack of vision that fails to develop a dependable stream of talented and well-trained young players also fails to recognize and appreciate outstanding budding talent when it is on hand. It can be difficult to identify and correctly assess an unproven youngster's ultimate potential, but it is critically important that the organization finds the people with the ability to do so.

This takes years of consistent, determined groundwork to attract, retain, and foster a cadre of experts with the facility to spot future stars. Like the farm system itself, a network of scouts and minor league managers and coaches doesn't just happen by accident. It requires investment, year after year, guided by judicious decision-making. And it demands a certain quantum of patience and long-view attitude on the part of management, lest a nascent superstar like Brock or Maddux escape to haunt his former organization for the remainder of a lengthy, glittering career.

Every leader must be alert to the fact that young team members are the future of the organization. To stay vibrant and competitive, every organization has to regularly mix sufficient new talent in with the older, more established individuals to ensure continued viability. As more mature employees retire, die, or depart for a different job, the leader must replace them...but this cannot be done without a great deal of careful planning and preparation. You don't just replace an experienced, valuable performer like you would change a light bulb. Leaders need to plan for the inevitable departures, some of which happen on a predictable timetable, and some of which come as a shock to everyone.

This is another aspect of the "law of the harvest." No organization can count on a ready and steady supply of new talent unless it first attracts, develops, and retains that talent. When leaders cannot or will not do what it takes to appraise, early and correctly, the raw potential of their newer workers, they are vulnerable to Brocking themselves.

Myopic leaders will be sitting ducks for their competitors, some of whom will be prepared to lure away the camouflaged prizes from talent hunters who can't see what's right in front of them. Those who spend the time and resources necessary to become shrewd judges of unrealized potential will cherry-pick the best from those who refuse to make such an investment. The harvest will be reaped by those prepared to separate the wheat from the chaff, and who hold onto the wheat. True, sometimes even the best professionals will make an erroneous assessment when it comes to young talent. It is a risky and uncertain enterprise, with no guarantees. But that is precisely why leaders must make every effort to get it right.

It is much better to hold onto a few young team members a bit too long, even when they never fulfill their apparent potential, than to make the opposite mistake and let a tremendous performer switch to the competitor's side just when he or she is ready to shine. The first error results in some wasted money, time, and effort, with the rewards not commensurate with the investment. But the second error yields a glaring example of the maxim "haste makes waste," by preemptively terminating ties to a developing star, who not only ceases contributing to the original team, but, even worse, actively devotes all that ability to the new team. The shortsighted leader thus doubles the self-inflicted damage, simultaneously losing a valuable long-term talent and throwing that talent into the lap of a close competitor. Ouch.

And if management eventually wakes up and realizes its serious talent shortage, how can a team replace the good, relatively inexpensive young stars that have slipped away? Often the only short-term possibility involves trying to hire proven performers away from other organizations; and established stars come attached to fancy price tags.

Just ask the Cubs of 2008, who paid a premium price to get the Japanese slugging outfielder Kosuke Fukudome to move halfway around the world to join the team—the polar antithesis of home-grown talent. When you can't develop your own talent, you must search far and wide to find it available elsewhere, and then pay top dollar (or bushel baskets full of dollars) to buy it from others, or just do without it. It's a matter of play, pay, or pray.

The Cubs wound up doing all three with Fukudome. To lure him away from Japan, the Cubs had to offer an immense four-year, $48 million contract. They hoped he would bring his famous power-hitting skills with him. But Fukudome's playing did not live up to all the paying and praying. During the Cubs' Division Championship season in 2008, in which they won more regular-season games than any other National League team, Fukudome struggled to produce an underwhelming .257 batting average, with just 10 home runs and 58 runs batted in. Although he got into 150 games, he was frequently sitting on the bench for crucial match-ups in the second half of the season while much less costly players took his place. One of the few silver linings in this fools-gold-plated example is that the late, great Cubs broadcaster Harry Caray, with his well-known penchant for mangling players' names, wasn't ever asked to try to pronounce Fukudome for the Cubs' millions of television viewers.

The flip side to this don't-Brock-yourself coin centers on the situation where it isn't the management that decides which young employees leave... it's the employees, one at a time. Some teams have a serious problem holding onto rising stars, and this is just as detrimental to the collective prospects for success as affirmatively discarding those future Most Valuable Players. We will call this situation the "reverse-Brock."

Many leaders are burdened with a blind spot when it comes to why good workers might tend to leave. The leaders might genuinely be unaware of drawbacks afflicting their own workplace; either they would rather not look for them, or they are too disengaged from conditions at the workers' level to perceive the situation's reality.

For managers who usually lounge within their own plush offices' cushy cocoon, and rarely associate with anyone but other upper-level administrators, they can easily assume that everyone in the entire place must have a very pleasant life indeed. Plus, they may be reluctant to dig for buried landmines, knowing they could be held responsible for placing them there, or leaving them unattended. Also, regardless of whether they actually had anything to do with creating or perpetuating the negatives, many leaders tend to take it personally when anyone suggests needed improvements. They see it as an assault on their worth as a person and their competence as a leader when someone offers any possible change in the status quo. But that is a leader's key quality: discontent with the status quo, desiring to change things and add value to the process of change. Leaders are compelled to alter the future state and make it better.

Blind-spot leaders often have a wall of invisible shields built up as a defense against "attacks" on their skills. They deride those who make suggestions, calling them whiners and chronic complainers, or spoiled brats who don't know how good they have it. In fairness, sometimes employees do pose their suggestions impolitely, or with some degree of anger and bitterness, and a leader may understandably feel under siege. But we risk preemptively shutting off all avenues of constructive criticism and useful ideas if we reflexively dismiss complaints, sarcastically asking the employees if they would like some cheese with their whine. Leaders who swat down suggestions as if being nipped by annoying mosquitoes communicate their attitude very clearly. All employees soon get the message: no reforms, suggestions, or criticisms are welcome in the leader's office. That creates a barren wasteland of ideas…an arid place for leaders to shrivel up and blow away.

With the good leader, the opposite is true. They value, appreciate, and encourage ideas from followers. To generate ideas, these leaders like to ask,

"What do you think?" and use the answers to help make other peoples' dreams come true, and improve the organization.

The leader can never overestimate the power of great questions: to seek more and better information. Asking rather than telling is becoming the key to leadership success. Leaders who lead with questions will create a more humane workplace, as well as a more successful organization. Good Cubs Fan leaders should be asking lots of open-ended questions to allow for better organizational creativity and improvement.

A Cubs Fan leader must not be afraid of frequent doses of reality therapy. If managers remain oblivious to persistent, recurring leakage—bright young talent draining out of the organization—they essentially acquiesce in bleeding their team dry. They need to run a periodic self-inspection, vigorously and thoroughly, to determine whether there is an issue of talent retention. Teams that hemorrhage top junior prospects cannot long remain competitive, especially since those prospects are generally heading straight for the competitors' hiring departments. One team's loss is quite literally another team's gain.

Question your personnel department, and talk with other leaders. Learn whether you have a problem involving a disproportionate number of the best newer or mid-career people voluntarily making an exit. If this voting-with-their-feet turns out to be a considerable phenomenon, it is time to root out the reasons why your Lou Brocks are jumping to your competitors.

For this process to work, you will have to involve people at all plateaus, from entry-level employee on up. If you fail to do this, and ask the wrong questions (or don't ask any questions at all), you will be incapable of gathering key information, and the problem will remain a mystery to you. You might choose to use an anonymous survey of all your people, perhaps supplemented with one-on-one interviews with some trusted employees at various levels. The precise method of data collection isn't nearly as important as your honest determination to discover the truth, no matter how unpleasant it may be.

To counteract the "reverse-Brock" syndrome (where top young prospects decide on their own to leave you for greener pastures, or something better than a pasture), you will want to examine in some detail why people leave, and what might be done to persuade them to stay. As the line from the film *Field of Dreams* says, "If you build it, he will come." The challenge: to pinpoint what to build to induce the best talent to come, and remain.

Don't assume you know all the reasons why people come and go. Take it from us—you don't! Ask the questions, and make sure they are the correct questions, and find out for certain. This is too important, so don't rely on unsupported unilateral assumptions and semi-educated guesses.

As you survey your people, truly attempt to place yourself in their situation, and identify with how they experience your workplace. This requires compassion, humility, empathy, creativity, and perceptiveness... maybe more of these commodities than we are accustomed to using on the job. But keep in mind that the individuals you want to attract and retain are different from you in significant respects. They are generally younger, more recently out of school, in a different family/social situation, more in need of money (often because of student loans), more technologically up-to-date, acclimated to a different learning environment from the one you knew, and much lower paid. These and other factors will make it challenging for you, the leader, to discern why such people come and go, and what might get them to stay.

Your organization won't move from good to great, or from lousy to mediocre, unless you can make it the type of place where the best young participants want to be. Naturally, a danger exists in over-generalizing, because each person responds to a unique set of conditions and incentives. No single combination of factors will prove ideal for everyone. There are as many sets of reasons why people stay or stray as there are people, with no two mosaics exactly identical.

Depending on individual needs, wants, and circumstances, some people will consider money far and away the predominant factor, while others may place much more emphasis on flexible hours and time off for family responsibilities. Some will insist on a low-stress, pleasant working environment, even if it comes with lower pay. Others crave being part of a hard-driving, mission-hungry team of devoted workers dedicated to achieving a worthy but elusive goal. Still other employees will need a convenient location with reliable public transportation, and will accept lower compensation. That can contrast to some of their co-workers who deem most important a favorable retirement plan and tax-deferred income options. Leaders are often surprised to learn about the variety of employment-related features that serve as the tipping point for employee

91

decisions on where to work; but they are only surprised if they make the effort to ask the right questions of the right people.

Virtually any one of the reverse-Brock items could rank first on any given employee's score sheet, contingent on their particularized family and personal context. That being said, it is productive to analyze trends and clusters of variables involving factors, such as those examples in the following list. Study them both in terms of your organization's offerings, and those of your closest competitors. You must consider both sides of this issue in great detail and specificity, objectively and realistically comparing your benefits with the other guys. Only then will you have any hope of improving your reverse-Brock situation.

We suggest making a chart or table where you can juxtapose your organization next to your main competition, along an array of reasonably-appropriate variables. Here is a list of some relevant, current, and acceptable work-related employee-satisfaction factors to get you started.

1. Salary/wages.

2. Opportunities for promotion.

3. Medical and dental insurance coverage.

4. Flexibility of working hours.

5. Workplace devoid of sexual harassment, bullying, hazing, or insults.

6. Freedom to work at home.

7. Congenial/fun working environment.

8. Convenience of location.

9. Opportunities to do interesting and challenging work.

10. Work that is important and worthy.

11. Retirement plan, including matching funds for 401(k) or 403(b).

12. Availability of good on-site childcare.

13. Generous leave policy for parents of new babies.

14. Workplace free of bias and promoting diversity related to race, sex, ethnicity, sexual orientation, religion, age, physical differences, and political views.

15. Official praise, honors, and recognition for good performance.

16. Attractive physical surroundings.

17. Vacation plan (number of days, flexibility).

18. Educational/training options.

19. Student-loan-repayment program.

20. Public-interest service opportunities.

21. Availability of bonuses and cash awards.

22. Prestige level of the organization.

23. Atmosphere welcoming creativity and innovation.

24. Quality and availability of computers, printers, scanners, video teleconferencing facilities, and other technology.

25. Career-broadening options.

26. Convenient, no-cost parking.

27. Employee-evaluation system that is both fair and perceived by the workers as fair.

28. Employer-funded travel and attendance at conferences, symposiums, and other gatherings.

29. Frequency and amount of pay increases.

30. Additional means of employee compensation (stock options, deferred compensation, etc.)

31. Adequacy of administrative support.

32. Number of work hours expected/demanded per day and per week.

33. Physical safety on the job.

34. Frequency of employer-mandated transfers to other locations.

35. Frequency of involuntary changes in duties and responsibilities.

36. Ability to work near where family members live.

37. Group camaraderie, cohesiveness, unity, and "team spirit."

38. Management's willingness to respond appropriately to employee ideas, concerns, and initiatives.

39. Co-workers who are trustworthy, admirable, respectable people.

40. Working environment of integrity, honesty, and fairness.

41. Management's treatment of all employees with dignity and respect.

42. General perception that the organization is headed in the right direction, with competent or better leadership, and a genuine chance to be the best.

43. Labor mostly free of needless paperwork, unproductive meetings, and purposeless administrivia.

44. Traffic problems getting to and from work.

45. Amount of pressure and tension perceived by people on the job.

46. Holidays.

47. Extent of internal competitiveness and cut-throat office politics within the team.

48. Amount of variety and freshness in the work to be done, versus monotonous repetitiveness.

49. Sense of mission and devotion to an important, noble cause within the organization.

As you evaluate your organization's relative pluses and minuses on these and other measures of employee satisfaction, you will see recurring patterns in people's views. It should become clear whether you have a reverse-Brock malady. It should also clarify what you can do about it.

Certainly, there are real-world constraints on every leader that limit what can and cannot be done. Some of these constraints might be alleviated through your own efforts, while others resist any movement. For example, the level of pay for each employee might be definitively determined by systemic structural realities literally beyond your control; this is typical of government jobs and many other large bureaucracies. The same may be true of work hours, vacation time, or retirement plans. But at a minimum, once you know what is causing your reverse-Brock, you have some chance of compensating for deficiencies in intractable areas with improvements in those areas where you do have some flexibility.

This is where your creativity, heavily supplemented by the creative input of your employees at all levels, becomes paramount. Once you are certain that a number of key factors cannot be changed, go down the rank-ordered list of the remaining factors; then think about what you *can* change, either to make negatives less of a drag, or to enhance existing positives even further.

Maybe you can't do anything dramatic about your location, salary structure, or medical plan, but you probably can make work more interesting, fun, creative, and cooperative. You can also ensure that everyone is afforded a full measure of dignity, politeness, respect, and equality. You may be able to adjust working conditions and hours, institute novel methods of rewarding exceptional performance, incentivize creative ideas, and reduce boring, mind-shutting drudgery.

Irrespective of how massive, ancient, and rigid your organization may be, even if it resembles one of those Easter Island statues on sedatives, there are always possibilities for positive transformation. These targets of opportunity come into view once you first methodically search for your organization's reverse-Brock factors, and then narrow your focus to the items within your broadest, most creative reach—the factors highly valued by your most valuable employees.

Your research will tell you in great detail what your people tend to see as most important to them, so you should be able to make positive changes in at least some of those categories. The very fact that you care enough to ask the questions and gather this information will impress some of your workers. Keep in mind that great questions empower people and instill in them a sense of their own strength and efficiency. When you are truly asking, you are sending the message that the followers' ideas are as good as or maybe even better than your own. And, armed with these ideas about your organization's advantages and detriments, you can more effectively develop, enhance, and publicize your selling points while doing all you can to ameliorate the minuses. Over time, this will show results in the number of Lou Brocks you attract, and keep under contract...and it never hurts to have a few more future Hall of Famers on your team, as long as the leader knows what to do with them.

5th Inning Discussion Questions

1. Does your organization have a sound mechanism for identifying promising young talent? What are traits leaders look for in assessing new talent in your field?

2. How can a leader judge when a worker is a "keeper" or not worth fighting over when other opportunities arise?

3. What are the pitfalls inherent in attempting to rate young performers at an early stage based on their supposed potential? How can leaders avoid these dangers?

4. How should leaders balance the competing needs of being fair to all workers while providing individualized incentives attractive enough to retain top performers?

5. To what extent does your organization measure, and pay attention to, the optimal facets of how employees produce, both individually and as a team?

6. Would your fiercest competitors fear the effectiveness of your talent acquisition and retention program? If so, why? If not, why not?

7. What metrics, or measures of performance, might be an improvement over those now used in your organization? Why aren't these already in effect? How can you put them into effect?

8. What are the primary loopholes in your organization's performance measurement mechanism that allow people to "game the system?" How could a leader remedy these defects? Why hasn't anyone already done this?

9. To what extent does your organization have a "reverse-Brock" problem? What are the primary causes?

10. Using the list in this book, supplemented by whatever other factors you deem appropriate, rate your organization's relative strengths and weaknesses in each employee satisfaction factor as compared to your three closest competitors.

6th Inning

Learn from Suffering, but Don't Learn to Love It

Which is worse: to be so prodigiously inept that you are consistently at or near the bottom of the standings, or to come close to winning the ultimate prize, only to have it vanish at the last instant? The Cubs and their fans are thoroughly acquainted with both of these species of pain, and both of them bring their own unique form of agony to the afflicted. This inning will analyze the origin and the antidote for each of these brands of losing.

When you are never in contention, the hurt is a persistent, low-level, life-numbing death of hope...or more precisely, dearth of hope, because no one ever expects to win in the first place. In this situation, the losing result is a foregone conclusion, and nobody expects anything else. A deep sense of fatalism sinks into the organization at all levels, with never dramatic highs or lows to upset the general despair. In a way, this variety of failure can prove less excruciating, because you're never disappointed, believing you had no chance to achieve anything in the first place. Losing becomes automatic. People learn to live with the monotonous funeral march of hopelessness, thinking little about it. Recognizing this, Winston Churchill said it best: "Success is going from failure to failure without loss of enthusiasm."

In contrast, a lot of success comes along for the ride with the other brand of losing. A team does very well for a long time, maybe for the entire regular season; it even reaches the postseason playoffs, winning many games, and giving many thrills to its members and followers. It might climb within sight of the ultimate championship, and be so near that the anticipatory taste of victory is on everyone's lips. Then, shockingly, horribly, disaster sweeps in and transforms joy into heartbreak. Defeat elbows triumph out of the way, and a stunning collapse enters the hall of legends.

The Cubs aren't the only team to suffer this type of loss. The Boston Red Sox have their own collection of endgame catastrophes too excruciating to mention for many of their fans. Other organizations also understand what it feels like to advance within touching distance of a championship before it turns into a mirage. This pain is sharper, deeper, and replete with an overdose of disappointment, all the more profound because it contrasts with all the success and hope that preceded it.

Thus the question of whether it is better to have loved and lost than never to have loved at all. The Cubs have experienced both syndromes repeatedly, and never rinsed away the sorrow with a championship champagne shower. So there is a natural tendency subconsciously to prefer the less severe, more comfortable pain of predictable, steady, low-impact incompetence. At least you can't have your heart broken when your heart isn't in it.

However, an optimistic outlook is an essential element of sound leadership. This is axiomatic. The belief that circumstances can improve, combined with the expectation that right actions will yield worthwhile rewards, is inextricably meshed with a leader's creativity, willingness to take chances, steadfastness in hard times, and ability to inspire others to achieve more than the ordinary.

The flip-side is that someone sitting in a boss's office who expects failure, views all change as threatening, and has no faith in a better future will be excessively risk-averse, and will lack both the impulse and the vision-spark necessary to lead a team beyond its inertia. The pessimist in leader's disguise is predisposed to a fatalistic attitude, and considers tragedy the inevitable ending for every comedy. Why seek innovation or try new programs when the ineluctable outcome can only be novel pathways to doom?

There is a natural oppression that repeated failure exerts on even normally optimistic people; and the Cubs have surely demonstrated this principle during their hundred years without a championship. You might indulge in a little pity-partying yourself if your organization had fallen short for ten consecutive demoralizing decades. The routine of ruin, the habit of haplessness, is the easy response to such spirit-numbing, protracted recycling of disappointment. An infinite loop of losing becomes very resistant to change when it has been making the same dismal rounds on the same route of routs for an entire century.

The Cubs have often been called "lovable losers." Thanks to the nationwide exposure they enjoy from their WGN Super Station cable and satellite television coverage, along with the gorgeous, ivy-adorned backdrop of their playing venue, historic Wrigley Field, this team has remained a profitable and popular attraction for many years—even those when their won-loss record resembled an accident report.

Perversely, some observers have suggested that the Cubs' popularity was sustained because of their losing ways, not despite them. Much like other famously inept teams such as the New York Mets of 1962, the Cubs may be so bad that people love them, taking them to heart as they would a helpless kitten. Indeed, why else would a sports team be named after a very young, clumsy, cute, harmless, cuddly, anything-but-fearsome ball of fur? In contrast to awe-inspiring team names along the lines of Tigers, Bears, Lions, Eagles, Falcons, Giants, and Titans, a team called the Cubs seems destined to be loved but not respected. Perhaps in life a value lingers beyond simply winning. This "love the Cubs syndrome" might be a reaction to the extreme pressure to win at any price, and fans have found something else to hold dear; maybe because they see in the Cubs a reflection of their own inadequacies.

As we stated at the outset of this inning, there are two main species of losing, and it is not surprising that the Cubs have had massive experience with both. Think about whether you have been involved with either or both forms of defeat during your life. If you have, consider what the effects were on you and others at all echelons of your organization, and what if anything pulled the group out of the failure mode.

One team variety, the *bottom scraper*, is characterized by consistently dismal non-competitiveness from start to finish. The team never approaches excellence and at no time comes within reach of the top of the crowd. The bottom-scraper approach offers no wrenching emotional swings and no sudden disappointments, because performance steadily remains at the same low level with only slight and temporary variations. Prolonged exposure to this environment leads to general depression, hopelessness, and listlessness. No one expects anything but ineptitude, stagnation, poor productivity, and failure, and that is exactly what the team delivers, like clockwork with a broken clock.

The other losing mode, the *roller coaster*, features tantalizing brushes with victory, and even extended periods at the pinnacle of achievement, ultimately punctured by one or more plunges into final defeat. When you're on a roller coaster ride, your emotions prove much more volatile than with a bottom scraper; hopes naturally rise when the group is doing well, and there are delicious hints of a big prize. The thrills of collective excellence get your adrenaline gushing and your dreams multiplying as you flirt with triumph. You experience fun times and the promise of continued success, even a championship. Such optimistic winged hopes inflict intense pain when they are eventually dragged down hard, clawing and biting, into the pit of the vanquished. The contrast between elation and despair is jarring, and the final sad result becomes immensely intensified because it is so different from the sunny prelude.

Vast stretches of nowhere seasons have haunted the Cubs, years in which the only question remained: How deep in last place will they finish? This disease has plagued them for much of their history, since FDR was in the White House. For example, from 1946 to 1963, the Cubs finished dead last in six seasons, and only managed to win more games than they lost (a very modest definition of "winning season") a mere three times. They managed—or mismanaged—to amass no seasons at all with a win rate above 50 percent between 1973 and 1983, while ending up in last place four times. This bottom-scraper syndrome was even worse than it first appears: During several years since 1961, the only teams bearing worse records were brand-new expansion franchises populated entirely with raw rookies and rejects from other teams. The Cubs are very well acquainted with the view at or near the basement.

The Cubs' roller coaster seasons remain far fewer in number but much more memorable (or harder to erase despite years of therapy). These years include several trips to the World Series as National League pennant-winners without a World Championship to show for it. This happened with surprising regularity between 1929 and 1945, but never again since the end of World War II. Pennants flew aloft Wrigley Field in 1929, 1932, 1935, 1938, and 1945, with defeat in the World Series in every instance. No one knew, when the Cubs fell just short of a world title in 1945, that they would never again win so much as a National League championship pennant during the next 60-plus seasons. But they have delivered terrible disappointments within reach of a league pennant (as in 1984, 1989, 1998,

2003, 2007, and 2008) as well as searing near-misses at divisional titles (see especially 1969).

In one sense, the outcome smells equally bad whether you get there via the very different paths of the bottom scraper or the roller coaster: no top prize, no group success, no collective awards in either case. So does it matter which road you take if you end up at the identical destination? Is one species of losing better or worse than the other? As we have seen, Cubs fans have had plenty of opportunity to debate this issue. There's no facile answer. It really hinges on whether you believe heartbreak is preferable to hopelessness, and whether you find it more feasible to recover from one than the other. A Cubs Fan leader must understand the distinctions, and know how to get a team out of either losing trap.

With a team in bottom-scraper mode, group-stink often begets a group-think that accepts failure. It is perniciously easy to become mired in the mud at the murky lowest levels of any hierarchical system. Nothing is clear there except that nothing is changing much. One day, one month, and one year is indistinguishable from those before and, by all indications, those still to follow. It's all so steady, predictable, monotonous, boring, and…somehow comfortable. When no one really expects anything good to happen, it's hard to be disappointed. The fetid productivity was anticipated from the beginning, and this was never punctuated by any indications to the contrary. So the only emotional reaction becomes a dull sensation of pointlessness and resignation. The group surrenders its dreams in exchange for empty sleep. It's certainly not a good feeling, but it lacks the acute piercing impact a dramatic crash from hopefulness provokes. Bottom-scraper pain is more like a persistent nagging headache than the agony of a roller coaster's fractured skull.

Yet a roller coaster does have its benefits. The wild ride has ups, not just downs. There are cheers along with tears, not just an uninterrupted yawn-fest. The performance chart isn't only a flat line always hugging the lowest edge, but rather a varied EKG of activity reflecting vital evidence of life. There are flirtations with a winning experience, and these side-trips to success can supply a very tasty appetizer that leaves people salivating, wanting much more. The team gains some appreciation of what it takes to excel during its time at or near the top, and a good leader can use that as the seed for more extended success. Hopes, even when dashed, can sometimes be revived if the leader properly nurtures the remnants, and helps the team learn the right lessons from the roller coaster ride. But how is the leader to move everyone to own the best of the experience, committing to building on that positive foundation, and not to yield to the belief that disaster is fated to repeat itself?

One key to unlocking a team from its roller coaster cell is the proper use of the equation we discussed in our 4th Inning. The Coefficient of Panic Vulnerability (C.P.V.) can be particularly high (that is, bad) for a group that has suffered a devastating crash. Those who live through such a disaster sometimes learn the wrong lessons from that trauma, and become excessively risk averse, fearful, and pessimistic. A leader who knows how to steer the C.P.V. in a positive direction will provide the antidote the team needs to move beyond its shock and pain, and grow better prepared to overcome the next set of challenges.

A catastrophe often brings with it the embryonic potential for phoenixlike rebirth. The organization will flourish if a leader skillfully orchestrates the various factors reflected in the team's C.P.V. to derive the best-glowing embers from all those ashes. As its C.P.V. trends lower, the team will become both increasingly capable of harnessing the talents and abilities that had brought it near the top before, *and* more resistant to any recurrence of the previous downfall.

With a bottom-scraper, rut-bound group, a leader faces a different array of obstacles and opportunities. As opposed to the roller coaster's emergency-room panic, this type of situation produces a persistent low-level negative situation, free from the often-damaging trauma produced by crashing aspirations. With hopes that have never been given wings, and thus have never suffered the hurt of a hard fall, it can prove easier to urge them to fly. It takes talent and work to break everyone loose from the familiar muck, but with the right inspiration it can be done. The very novelty of—at last—a leader who refuses to accept continued losing can sometimes awaken long-dormant energies. This group will need to be taught how to win, and to shed some long-established habits of defeat; but it won't have to overcome agonizing memories of recent collapses where apparent victory cruelly and suddenly vanished.

Let's look a little closer at what this entails. Organizations have personalities, just as do individuals, and it is possible for an organization to acquire a collective mentality content with mediocrity. It often stems from a perverse, dysfunctional system of rewards and accountability. When plentiful money continues to flow in regardless of performance, then the incentives to work hard, develop new skills, and learn better methods become severely undermined. This is exacerbated if there are no penalties for poor effort, or results in the form of public disapproval, stigma, damage to reputation, and the like.

Some economists are fond of pointing out that, when we subsidize something, we get more of it; and when we penalize something, we get less of it. Basic human nature often responds to such carrots and sticks; but when the incentives and disincentives are improperly dispensed, people may well give us more of what we don't want and less of what we desire.

In a sick environment, incentives and disincentives are seriously misaligned. The Cubs have long existed within a sick environment where paid attendance, team salaries, television revenue, merchandising income, celebrity status, and fan support remained steady—or even grew—almost entirely independent of how well the team actually performed.

Because performance has been divorced from consequences, the system suffocates potential reforms with an overwhelming impulse not to fix what isn't broken...with "broken" defined as significant loss of tangible rewards rather than loss of championships. This sick environment keeps the goodies coming at a generous level, whether the team wins or loses, and asks little more from the team beyond just showing up, and maybe making things interesting with a few notable individual achievements. When a losing attitude, careless performance, half-hearted effort, and lack of initiative are tolerated at worst and celebrated at best, many people grow comfortable with mediocrity. The sick environment is not a blessing in disguise, but rather a curse in the disguise of a blessing. It induces the view, "Why not mail it in when the checks continue to arrive in the mail anyway?"

If you are trying to lead an organization burdened with a sick environment, it can feel like running through quicksand with a heavy backpack. A self-starter with a strong internal need to achieve seems like an alien visitor in a place where rewards are uncoupled from performance, bad is "not bad," and good means whatever minimum it takes to keep the benefits flowing. People who enjoy a pleasant, well-compensated lifestyle within the sick status quo may strongly resent and resist any suggestion that change is necessary. Change could remove rewards for poor productivity, making promotions and pay contingent on objectively demonstrable accomplishment. The result: a rude shock for those who have long been perfectly content to make the system work for them rather than vice versa.

The leader who decides that things are broken and need fixing will not be welcomed by the many whose comfort and security are threatened by any move to link actions to consequences. People who are gently breast-fed by a sick system will not want to deal with a world that demands more from them than staying alive.

If a team like the Cubs can be adored by millions of rabid followers, and reliably garner huge sums of money from television, merchandizing, and ticket sales while never winning a World Championship—and indeed while often losing more games than it wins in a given season—it may understandably feel less than a sense of urgency concerning the need to change. Maybe these tangible rewards would be even greater if the team actually won, but who knows? And who knows whether the increased rewards, if any, would be worth the extra sacrifices it would take to get there? Perhaps the marginal costs of devoting additional time, effort, and resources would not justify the incremental gains that might be derived from them, speaking from a purely cost-benefit perspective. And when it is realized that—even if the organization made major changes and invested huge amounts of treasure and work in improving—no guarantee exists that this would lead to ultimate success, the accountant's balance sheet becomes all the more uncertain. In this connection, it makes sense to remember Casey Stengel's famous dictum: "Making predictions is always difficult, particularly when they're about the future."

Once tangible rewards are subtracted from a team's reasons to improve, all that remains are things such as pride in excellence, determination to perform at the highest possible level, competitive spirit, need for achievement, and a moral sense that it is wrong to accept undeserved accolades or unearned pay. Some people are motivated by these intangible, psychic considerations, and will not be satisfied with mediocrity even if they know they could easily get by with less than full effort. Other people need that no-kidding, bottom-line inducement to spur them to work hard and produce; and if that incentive is missing, they will be perfectly content to do whatever bare minimum is actually required of them. The same is true for teams and organizations of all types and at all levels.

How does an incentive-poor syndrome get started? In some contexts, arguably real advantages become associated with underdog status. Many people have a natural tendency to root for the underdog, maybe because they identify with the world's have-nots, has-beens, and was-nots. This inclination has been cultivated in countless works of popular culture, from comic books to comic operas, in variations on the rags-to-riches theme. So underperforming teams might attract a disproportionate share of public sympathy and support, increasing in inverse relation to their success rate.

More practically, underdogs are often under a minimum of pressure. Once their status as underdogs is confirmed in the eyes of their customers, employers, or viewers, the underdogs can tread water for a long time in the shallow, tepid wading pool of low expectations. This requires relinquishing normal competitive urges and impulses to excel. Given an environment where mediocrity is nurtured, people can come to enjoy a situation where no one demands much from them. It's a bit like preschool for adults, where grades run the whole gamut from "awesome" to "zowie" and constructive criticism consists of nuanced forms of ooh and aah. Like doting parents who enthuse over every masterpiece in tempera from their toddlers' paintbrushes, authority figures coddle underdogs within an atmosphere where the slightest accomplishment is acclaimed. It's virtually impossible to fail in such a setting, and the near-unconditional adulation and overflowing praise-trays can be seductively addicting. If minimal standards suffice, no refrigerator door is big enough to display all the instant Gainsboroughs.

It's a sick mentality that breeds this disorder, but those who succumb derive a measure of comfort from the lack of people pestering them for the latest statistics. When the Cubs are nestled near the bottom of the standings, you don't get asked what the score was 12 times every day. It is something of a relief, in a way. There's no need to get too nervous or upset about the day-to-day activities, because no one expects much of anything to happen, other than more of the same steady, bland, low-spice rations of mush. Why look over your shoulder if you're already dead last? You expect to lose most of the time, and everyone inside and outside the organization shares the same outlook; so there's a very low disappointment risk. There's nothing to lose when losing is the norm, and everyone is benchmarking off of a standard of universal acceptance where groups are treated as if they were above average irrespective of quality. Who boos at a kindergarten talent show? What critic writes a scathing review panning the stars of a beginners' dance showcase? Where the "underdog understanding" is underfoot, the only quasi-requirement is just showing up.

The underdog understanding rewards the slightest evidence of talent, the least scintilla of production. A sprinkling of individual achievement mixed in with an occasional momentary team victory is sufficient to keep the support coming. After all, what more could you expect from an underdog beyond sporadic glimpses of good through the fog of everyday good-enough?

If the system itself is counterproductive, showering abundant money, praise, status, and perquisites on us irrespective of our effort and performance, the leader has a knotty problem. How does a leader cut through the tangled and twisted strands of such a dysfunctional system and motivate people to demand more of themselves? This is a real challenge in fields far removed from the Cubs' seemingly unique status of lovable losers, where underdog understandings have developed for a variety of reasons.

For example, some governmental bureaucracies are notorious for failing to adequately incentivize high achievement or punish/eliminate slackers, resulting in prodigious levels of inefficiency and waste, lack of customer service, poor work quality, low employee morale, stagnant productivity, minimal innovation, and massive institutional inertia. Educational establishments can also divorce performance from accountability, such as when tenured professors are barely expected to produce anything to justify their considerable salaries and comfortable lifestyles. The predictable consequence: a number of senior professors who rarely show up for work, publish nothing, and pay little attention to their minimal teaching duties.

The Cubs have often exemplified an organization where incentives and culture are not in line with an objective measure of success or productivity. Both at the organizational and individual level, it has been entirely possible to make piles of money and enjoy popular support, affection, and even adulation without producing the championships (or even the winning record) that normally would warrant such rewards. Quite naturally, the impetus for positive change is largely neutralized when generous tangible and intangible benefits continue to flow uninterrupted despite prolonged doldrums of lackluster efforts and results.

History has certainly taught us that human beings are not entirely rational creatures. To a significant extent, though, we do respond to incentives and disincentives in fairly predictable ways. One of the most formidable obstacles any leader can face is an environment—whether a team, an organization, a political entity, or any other group of people—where a vulture culture has sunk its claws deep into the soft tissue.

A vulture culture gets by on the scraps and leftovers that remain behind when productive activities have stopped. When leaders and team members behave as if it's good enough to scrape out an existence from rotten carrion and lifeless carcasses, despite the stench and ignominy, who can expect much progress? We've all seen this in one form or another. The Cubs have had profitable seasons when they played to large crowds, just by making losing look interesting.

Some systems have made the tacit assumption that mediocrity is better than meritocracy, that winning isn't everything and that self-esteem must be propped up at all costs. There are pass/fail structures in place far beyond academe, where everything passes for passing and real excellence passes right by. Within a milieu dedicated to the notion that success sucks, people act as if living in a perpetual youth soccer game, where no one keeps score and the outcome is forever a nothing-to-nothing draw. This type of vulture culture is sometimes described by phrases such as "getting over," "getting by," or "if the minimum weren't good enough it wouldn't be the minimum."

Some observers believe that such an anti-achievement, mediocrity-mired attitude is disproportionately represented among today's young people. The theory maintains that the "Millennium Generation" of students and employees was brought up in an overly supportive, judgment-free atmosphere where criticism was virtually unknown, and demandingly high standards were conspicuously absent. Given such a rigor-deficient formative experience, where the insistence on rigor is in *rigor mortis*, it would be natural if people tended to be content with much less actual productivity in both quantity and quality.

Regardless of whether the rising generation is unusually prone to fall into the vulture-culture trap, it remains true that no one is entirely safe. Irrespective of age, race, ethnicity, socio-economic status, generational affiliation, gender, geographical origin, or any other factor, human beings can be affected, and infected, by the contagious and dangerous sick-culture syndrome. No leader should assume that people from *any* category are necessarily subject to or immune from vulture-culture tendencies.

Societal structures along the lines of socialism, or the welfare system in the United States prior to the Clinton-era reforms, are a large-scale example of what happens when incentives are eliminated, greatly reduced, or even pull in the wrong direction. The joke in the former Soviet Union under communism had a typical worker saying, "They pretend to pay us and we pretend to work."

People tend to be adept at figuring out how to operate, within whatever system applies to them, to get the most benefits for themselves in exchange for the least amount of personal discomfort, at least in the short run. We may not behave rationally and logically in all areas, and we may not be very good at discerning long-term consequences, but collectively we can often find our path of least resistance and most reward. If the system rewards out of wedlock births, or pays about the same amount for inactivity as it does for full-time work at the type of jobs generally available, or fails to monitor and deal effectively with differential levels of productivity, it should not be surprising that many people will respond in the way most convenient, comfortable, and lucrative for themselves. That doesn't mean that they are lazy, selfish, manipulative, unwise, or immature...only that they are responding to an imperfect system in a way that seems to be best for them and their families, at least in the absence of skilled leadership to reverse the system's powerful downward gravitational pull.

Such perverse systemic incentives usually take many years to become firmly established. They come about through the gradual accretion of well-intentioned employee benefits, provisions for job security, safeguards against capricious management methods, economic safety nets for poverty-stricken children, compassion for the poor, ideals of academic freedom, union negotiations, egalitarian principles, and the absence of strong forces pulling in the opposite direction. They are facilitated by some of the less admirable but nonetheless widespread and understandable facets of human nature. A leader might feel like a modern Hercules asked to clean out the stinking Augean stables. Where to begin? What tools might be available to clear out such a vast and longstanding mess?

One possibility is to alter the system's incentive/disincentive structure to more appropriately reward the desired behaviors and penalize the actions and attitudes we want to reduce. Few leaders have the unilateral power to work this type of systemic change, because the structure is imposed by law, or maintained by a mighty network of senior officials who personally profit from the status quo. It might be more feasible in a small organization, or, given sufficient autonomous authority in the individual leader, in a subcomponent of a larger organization (branch, office, division, etc.). But usually it will not be possible for even the best leader to transform a well-entrenched system of counterproductive incentives, both because of basic institutional inertia and the self-interest of many in maintaining the existing scheme.

It is also usually the case that the organization could use some addition by subtraction: getting rid of Trojan horses who do more from within to harm than to help. But again, these problem people are often protected by systems that provide near-impregnable job security, and sometimes by powerful allies within the organization. They may command large salaries and a legion of admirers, the legacy of past glories that the now-unproductive person is using to coast by on autopilot. Or they may just be very good at knowing how to game the system and build a mutual-protection network for like-minded place-holders. Many sports teams, governmental bureaucracies, and established corporations suffer under the burden of this condition. In such a setting, a leader can be almost powerless to jettison dead wood, even when it is clearly functioning only as kindling to burn down the whole structure from within.

So what can a leader do if the system itself is corrupt, and people who should be fired nonetheless remain invulnerable? It is possible, though still not easy by any means, that the leader—sometimes the same leader with a new approach, or, more often, a new leader with a different take on the situation—can catalyze a shift in attitude and culture, both on an individual and institutional level. Just as there are fundamental components of human nature that make people susceptible to the allure of a dysfunctional incentives system, there are other core elements common to all people that yearn for more noble ideals. A leader might explore ways of tapping into these loftier aspects of every personality, beginning by effectively and continually demonstrating these traits through the leader's own actions and behavior.

A recent example of this came during Lou Piniella's first season as manager of the Cubs. On June 2, 2007, Piniella was watching in disgust as his team sank toward its sixth consecutive loss (and 10th out of its last 12 games). The Cubs were fighting among themselves more aggressively than they were against the guys in the other dugout; just the day before Piniella had to break up an angry scuffle between Cubs pitcher Carlos Zambrano and Cubs catcher Michael Barrett. Now, in the 8th inning of an eventual 5-3 loss to the Atlanta Braves, the manager went wild in front of the hometown Wrigley Field fans.

Piniella's tantrum was nominally triggered by a questionable call from third-base umpire Mark Wegner, but it really was secretly directed at his own players. Sweet Lou knew in advance that he was going to be ejected from the game and fined, so he made sure it was worth it. He used his feet like a cartoon character on speed, kicking dirt all over Wegner's shoes and then booting his own cap several times. Piniella played his "mad scene" like Lady MacBeth in baseball drag, making certain that he finally was dragged away, neck veins bulging, by another umpire. But the real point wasn't the umpire's decision. The Cubs' new leader knew his listless, divided collection of individuals needed to get fired up about something other than their own statistics and their own petty internal squabbles. The best, and maybe the only, way to do that was to lead by example—and a dramatic, unmistakable example at that.

He wanted his players to see their leader going absolutely pegged-out berserk over a rather routine umpiring call in yet another rather routine losing game. He wanted his disheartened, disillusioned gaggle of separate prima donnas to see, in livid color, their leader pouring his heart and guts into a minor part of a nothing-special game. After the contest was over, Piniella admitted to reporters that the umpire's decision was correct, but that he had previously made up his mind to blow up no matter what. The heart of the matter was a matter of heart. The Cubs, like their manager, needed to start caring about their collective success, as a team, and caring enough to show it, big-time. Piniella's tirade worked, and many traced the Cubs' success for the remainder of the 2007 regular season to the manager's well-planned, well-timed, outrageous, outsized outburst.

Additionally, the Cubs' fiery new manager knew that some personnel problems require more than a kick in the pants. He quickly and permanently solved the Zambrano-Barrett issue by sending the combative catcher to another team where Barrett could have a fresh chance to figure out the mystery of whether the bad guys were wearing his own uniform or that of the opposing team.

We may not always show it, but all of us possess within ourselves certain profoundly significant and positive human characteristics. We need to be needed. We need to be valued, both for who we are and for the good things we do. We need to feel that our lives have meaning beyond the mundane minutiae of daily survival. We need to believe that what we do makes a difference for the better in some way—that our work is important and valuable. We need to feel that we are not alone in what we do, but rather are part of a team that is devoted to something bigger and more vital that just our own narrow, selfish pursuit of cash. We need to believe that whatever good we accomplish will not die with us, but will live on to make the world better for someone. We need to have something to be justifiably proud of, something we have helped achieve. We need to be something better than the perennial underdog, and have a shot at becoming top dog. And we need to be busy, not for the sake of killing time, but in the cause of something that matters in a positive way.

Even in the belly of a beast that seemingly has forgotten—if it ever knew—what its purpose is, a leader can try to spark these latent needs. This cannot be done while cowering behind a desk. The leader must be very visible in demanding only the very best, beginning with the leader's own output and outlook. If "good enough" isn't good enough for the leader in his or her self-appraisal, then maybe "close enough for government work" will cease to be the rallying cry of the inert masses at all other levels of the organization. A leader who accepts blame and responsibility, who never settles for less than excellence from himself or herself, and who never stops trying to improve, will at least be a good example to anyone around who is awake. Someone might notice that there is no room for the status quo in the leader's own status, and that might just be the beginning of positive change in people other than the leader.

If the leader cannot clear away the dead wood, and cannot bring it back to life, then it could be time to do whatever is within the leader's power to make the slackers responsible for their poor performance. Good old-fashioned wall-to-wall counseling can supply a galvanizing shock to the system for long-inactive brains, and to those who are watching from the sidelines. Confrontation is unpleasant, but so is losing, and it can help turn things around if the leader succeeds in making losing unpleasant for everyone who contributed to bringing about the defeat. A well-deserved kick in the pants can send a message clear enough for even the most lethargic observer to comprehend.

Leaders can also sometimes withhold benefits and perquisites, even if they are unable to fire or cut the salaries of unproductive employees. The consistent message must be that weak effort, laziness, sloppy work, absenteeism, malingering, time wasting, and apathy are no longer the ingredients of a comfortable and happy work environment. When the Big Dog gets fed up, the underdogs will have to wake up. Mailing it in is only something people can do if they want to tender their resignations.

6th Inning Discussion Questions

1. Is the incentive/disincentive system in your organization encouraging the correct behaviors and levels of performance? In what ways might this system be improved?

2. Why do people, and groups of people, become satisfied with poor performance?

3. If a new leader joins an organization mired in a bottom-scraper, vulture culture of hopelessness, what are the top three actions that might turn things around?

4. What would change in your answer to question number 3 if the leader is coming into a roller coaster team instead of a bottom scraper?

5. How does an attitude such as "close enough for government work" become entrenched in an organization?

6. What are five indicators that can tell a leader when a particular employee has given up and is merely going through the motions?

7. Do you personally believe it is preferable to get very near to the pinnacle of achievement, only to fall short at the end, or to remain comfortably and consistently in back of the pack throughout? What are the top three reasons for your answer?

8. What would be your workers' view of the preceding issue? Why do most of them hold that opinion? Is this a problem? What could be done to generate positive change?

9. Can a new leader realistically hope to transform an "underdog understanding" vulture culture where people are encouraged just to get by and not to achieve anything beyond what is minimally required?

10. What one word best captures the essence of your organization's employee-performance evaluation system? What is the single most important initiative that might improve that system?

11. When employees are retained, paid, and promoted despite lackluster performance and poor attitude, what is the effect on the organization?

7th Inning
Blame Doesn't Win the Game

At times it appears that the Cubs have taken every setback as an opportunity to blame others. When they lose important games, when pennants and seasons dissolve in adversity's acid, Cubs players and managers tend to point fingers at each other, at other teams, the umpires, fans, television announcers, the newspapers, the weather, at mystical curses…at anyone but the Cub in the mirror.

This is a coping mechanism most of us master as toddlers, because of its dual comforting effects: It relieves us from responsibility while simultaneously "telling on" someone else, getting them in trouble. When bad things happen to good people, it feels good to tell everyone who will listen that it isn't our fault. We are innocent victims, the mistreated good guys betrayed by malevolent villains, bad luck, and nature's forces beyond our control.

At its most virulent, blame is directed at one's own teammates or manager. During the 1969 season, the Cubs found a way to squander a huge nine-and-a-half game lead over the New York Mets (eight-and-a-half over the then second-place Cardinals) with only about six weeks left to play. In a stunning turnaround, the Cubs actually ended the season eight games behind the Mets—a swing of 17 games in the closing few weeks. Blame was a major ingredient in the Cubs' recipe for disaster, along with liberal doses of panic, premature assumption of victory, and other leadership landmines. Indeed, the Cubs turned 1969 into a veritable greatest-hits album of how not to win.

The blame game first began eroding the Cubs' successful year as early as July 8. On that day with the great Ferguson Jenkins pitching, the Cubs took a 3-1 lead into the 9th inning against the Mets in New York. The Cubs lost a game they should have won when rookie centerfielder Don Young misplayed two balls in the field. Neither play was ruled an error, but the floodgates opened nonetheless. The Mets defeated the Cubs 4-3, scoring the winning run on Young's second miscue. A painful loss, it was still only one game in midseason, and the Cubs remained far in front in the standings. It should have been only a momentary minor setback, but key senior Cubs members transformed it into something infinitely worse.

After the game, manager Leo Durocher and star third baseman Ron Santo publicly excoriated Don Young in front of both the team and reporters. Durocher was quoted as snarling, "My three-year-old could have caught those balls!" He reportedly griped, "That kid in center field! He botched one ball and gave up on the other!" Rather than dealing with the loss as the team effort it was, or at least maintaining a semblance of team unity and mutual support, the Cubs gave new meaning to the cliché "I've got your back."

After team leaders blatantly betrayed one of their own, and one of their most junior teammates at that, an ulcer infected the Cubs' heart. Further rounds of recrimination and dissension ensued. The Cubs were no longer a team, just an aggregation of individuals who happened to wear the same uniform, each watching out for himself and wondering when the blame would be dumped on him. A golden opportunity for a pennant-winning season began gradually crumbling in a heap of pointing fingers.

The Cubs' fortunes deteriorated to the point where they resorted to blaming their downfall on supernatural curses and hexes. Tension mounted as their once-immense lead melted like ice on an August sidewalk. Their decline culminated in an infamous incident on Sept. 9 in a game against the Mets at Shea Stadium, New York. The previous day, the Mets had dealt the Cubs a gut-punch loss centered on a controversial photo-finish play at the plate in which Tommy Agee was ruled safe, scoring a key run for the Mets. Cubs' catcher Randy Hundley was so outraged by the umpire's call that he jumped high in the air like Donald Duck in catcher's gear, screaming furiously at the official…in vain, of course. The Mets won the argument and the game. But, astonishingly, the worst still lay just ahead.

In the second half of this crucial two-game match-up between the arch rivals, it took something even more otherworldly to beat the Cubs. A black cat wandered onto the field while the Cubs were at bat. The mysterious feline walked around Ron Santo (who was standing in the on-deck circle waiting to hit), then approached the Cubs' dugout and hissed at Leo Durocher. Although the Cubs had their ace Ferguson Jenkins pitching (just as during the Don Young incident), they lost the "black cat" game in gut-wrenching fashion, and fell out of first place the next day. They never got back.

Some eyewitness (and nose-witness) observers claimed that the dark, diabolical feline suffered from a severe case of body odor. Even if such catty aspersions are true, it's doubtful whether enhanced hygiene or liberal application of cologne and deodorant would have altered the streaking/stinking incident's aftermath. It wasn't the smell from the kitty that doomed the Cubs; it was the rotting stench of dead confidence.

The Cubs continued to lose at an appalling rate for the remainder of the year, scraping together a mere eight wins during all of September against 17 defeats. The Mets seemed to catch many lucky breaks, while the Cubs suffered from a prodigious run of bad luck. Many in Chicago attributed this to the black cat and the ill fortune it brought. It couldn't have been the Cubs' costly errors, weak bullpen, poor speed, faltering pitching, internal dissension, inadequate stamina, and lack of clutch hitting.

Curses have absorbed a disproportionate share of the blame for the Cubs' remarkable record of wrecks since at least Oct. 6, 1945, during the Cubs' last trip to the World Series. On that myth-making date, Chicago restaurant/tavern owner William "Billy Goat" Sianis and his pet goat Murphy were allowed into Wrigley Field for the fourth game of the World Series against the Detroit Tigers. Mr. Sianis actually had two choice box seat tickets, one for himself and one for his goat.

After getting into the stadium but before the game began, Sianis and Murphy made their way onto the field, causing a general uproar. The ushers intervened and wanted to escort the daring duo out of the park entirely; but after some argument, they permitted Sianis and the goat to occupy their seats. The peculiar pair watched the first three innings of Game Four, with Murphy, like the devoted Cubs fan he was, sporting a blanket with a note pinned to it reading "We Got Detroit's Goat."

Then, during the 4th inning of the big game, Cubs owner Philip K. Wrigley ordered both Billy Goat and real goat ejected from the ballpark due to the foul odor (from the true goat, not Mr. Sianis). Sianis was so enraged that, according to legend, he placed a curse on the Cubs that they would never again win a National League pennant or play in a World Series game at Wrigley Field. After the Cubs lost that game and eventually the World Series, the vengeful Mr. Sianis sent Mr. Wrigley a telegram bearing the famous rhetorical question, "Who Smells Now?"

Sianis and his Billy Goat Tavern went on to enjoy many years of fame and prosperity. They even became the inspiration for the renowned "cheezborger, cheezborger" *Saturday Night Live* "Olympia Restaurant" comedy skits on television featuring Bill Murray, Dan Aykroyd, and the late John Belushi.

Ever since 1945, the Cubs have had a ready excuse whenever their hopes turned hopeless. They have well rehearsed the script: "Who do you blame? Voodoo!" Alas, Sianis's curse on the Cubs has proved every bit as successful and enduring as his "cheezborgers," though decidedly harder for Cubs fans to swallow.

Believe it or not, during the ensuing 60 years the Cubs tried various schemes to remove the "Billy Goat Curse." They included formal apologies; invitations to Sianis family members and their goats to return to Wrigley Field; public pilgrimages to the ballpark by other goats and their human companions; intricate anti-curse ceremonies in Wrigley Field; official retractions of the curse by both the original "cursor" William Sianis (in 1969!) and his nephew Sam Sianis (on *The Tonight Show* with Jay Leno), and other outrageous hex-busting rituals. If the Cubs had put that much effort into building a great farm system instead of bringing goats from the farm, the results might have proved better.

Given the Cubs' long obsession with curses, we have often wondered why no one has drawn the obvious conclusion: The Cubs are blocked from winning another World Series by alien forces from outer space. As Casey Stengel was fond of saying, "You could look it up." The Cubs have not won another World Championship after their consecutive titles in 1907 and 1908.

Couldn't the reason be alien invasion? Think about it. The same year the Cubs hoisted their final World Champions banner, a 200-foot-wide meteor exploded five miles above the ground near Tunguska, Siberia. On June 30, 1908, the fireball's force hit the Earth with the power of 15 million tons of TNT, thousands of times greater than the force of the atomic bomb dropped on Japan in 1945. The colossal blast and ensuing inferno leveled some 1,200 square miles of forest. Shouldn't curse addicts wake up and recognize that the meteor was deliberately aimed at us by malevolent aliens and, although it hit the wrong side of the planet, it also knocked out all chances of any future Cubs World Championships for at least a century? The mother of all bean balls left quite an aftershock…one hundred years' worth.

Well, why not? After all, the alien attack theory makes about as much sense as the Billy Goat Curse.

In any event, the blame-misdirection and curse-reversal business continues to thrive in Chicago. Remember the freakish incident that touched off the Cubs' ruination in Game Six of the 2003 League Championship Series? The hapless Cubs fan Steve Bartman who got in the way of Moises Alou as he was trying to catch a foul popup? That instantly became the magnet for all the outwardly-directed blame, anger, and vindictiveness in the Cubs' world. Thousands of livid fans in Wrigley Field launched a massive barrage of litter and obscenities at Bartman for several minutes, and he soon fled the ballpark surrounded by armed guards. When Bartman's identity and home address were immediately revealed on the Internet and in the news media, it appeared for a time that he might be in real danger. Hounded by reporters and threatened by hordes of blame-aiming Cubs fans, Bartman had his phone disconnected and began hiding, afraid to go to work.

Even the ill-fated Illinois Governor Rod Blagojevich went so far as to tell the press that Bartman "better join the witness-protection program." Few suspected at the time that Blagojevich would have been better off taking his own advice than publicly attacking one of his citizens. Multiple editorial cartoons showed Bartman in hiding with his supposed fellow reclusive mega-villains Osama bin Laden and Saddam Hussein. Bartman was considered a hero in Florida, and was actually offered asylum by Florida Governor Jeb Bush. To his credit, Bartman never ran away from his mistake, fought back, tried to capitalize on his notoriety, or did anything other than express sincere sorrow for the harm he had accidentally caused the team he loved so much.

So what actions did the Cubs and their fans take to derive some benefit, some constructive lessons learned, from their horrid meltdown? Many fans memorized the precise seat number which Bartman had occupied (Aisle 4, Row 8, Seat 113) as if it held the numerological key to exorcising pennant-snatching demons. But the most significant response was just a new version of the Billy Goat wreck-the-hex curse-antidote rituals. The fateful ball from the Bartman incident was sold at an auction in December 2003, purchased for $113,824.16 on behalf of Harry Caray's Restaurant. In an amazing example of post-modern mysticism, the Bartman Ball was publicly exploded at Harry Caray's on February 26, 2004. The ceremonial destruction took place amidst much fanfare and lengthy, elaborate procedures. After all, it isn't easy to eradicate a curse when you believe in its power. The man who'd bought the wretched baseball put it this way: "It's like the ring from *The Lord of the Rings* and we're kind of like Frodo, trying to get it over with." No Cubs fan, however, would have dreamed of describing the doomed ball as "my precious."

The symbolic curse-cleansing wizardry didn't end when the smoke from the detonation blew away into the Chicago night sky. In 2005, the pitiful earthly remains of the blown-up baseball were used by the restaurant as ingredients in a pasta sauce. The ball was boiled and the steam captured, distilled, and added to the sauce. As of this writing, the recipe has failed to catch on. And rather than eating their words of premature boasting or dining on a little humble pie, the Cubs ate the cursed baseball.

To this day, every time the Cubs are leading their division late in the season, or even ahead in a postseason series, swarms of reporters bring up questions about the continuing effects of the curse. Fans talk about reversing the curse. Normally rational managers, coaches, and players feel compelled to deny the reality of evil spells bedeviling the team. And the inevitable errors, missed opportunities, poor performances, and ill fortune that come to all teams are magnified a thousand-fold when they befall the Cubs in pressure situations.

All the talks of curses, prior swoons, historic folding acts, and infamous years such as 1945, 1969, 1984, 1989, 2003, and 2004 virtually forces negative thoughts and emotions onto professionals who weren't even part of any of those Cubs teams. It's as if all that bad history is surgically transplanted into the psyches of innocent newcomers, and the foul results have been replicated many times. With the wrong mindset it can seem that you are playing two teams: the one actually in the field against you, and the combined forces of every team that ever dealt you a bad beating. And part of this is another round of blame and counter-blame, Cubs style.

The curse issue was forced onto Cubs manager Lou Piniella near the end of the remarkable 2007 season, his first at the helm in Chicago. Piniella, a veteran of many seasons as a successful player and a championship-winning manager, was in the process of leading the Cubs to a rare worst-to-first achievement, vaulting from last place in their division in 2006 to first place just one year later. But when the Cubs lost some important games during the last week of the regular season, reporters bombarded the two-time Manager of the Year award-winner with pointed questions about the Cubs' curses and earlier failures.

The Curse Hearse kicked into stomp-on-the-gas-pedal overdrive during the National League Division Series when the Cubs fell to a surging young Arizona Diamondbacks team. Piniella—who had experienced World Championships both as a star player (with the Yankees, twice) and as a well-respected manager (with the Reds)—found himself publicly repeating the mantra, "There is no curse. There is no curse." Many Cubs fans refused to believe him, needing someone or something to blame for their early exit from the playoffs. To them it was irrelevant that no player on the 2007 team had even been born in the "black cat" year of 1969, let alone the "billy goat" year of 1945, nor that Lou Piniella himself was a mere two-year-old toddler at the time of the goat incident.

Curse denial actually seemed to make tensions worse for the 2007 Cubs as the National League Division Series took on ever more ominous overtones. Pessimism, pressure, constant reminders of ancient and recent debacles, and the withering spotlight of national media coverage combined to exert tremendous negative force on the players and manager alike, especially after the Cubs lost Game One under agonizing circumstances, 3-1.

The situation reached a memorable low point in the 2nd inning of Game Two when the Cubs' usually-reliable starting pitcher Ted Lilly surrendered a three-run homer to rookie Chris Young. The blast erased the Cubs' two-run lead formed only a few minutes earlier—their first lead of the series. Lilly was so overcome with frustration as the ball rocketed into the stands, he wound up and furiously flung his glove down into the dirt. If Lilly had thrown the last pitch to Young as hard as he threw his glove, the Cubs still might have been ahead. It was a display of unrestrained tantrum-level emotions usually found only on the most decrepit Little League fields. Even manager Lou Piniella had to admit that he'd never before seen anything like Lilly's histrionics during his many years in professional baseball. But that's what obsession with doom, gloom, and boom can do, even to veteran professionals. The crushed Cubs went on to lose the series to Arizona in three straight games, scoring a meager total of six runs in the entire series.

Might as well look to the usual suspects and blame it on the curse, right? The Cubs, like many of us, found it more comfortable to cry about their curse than to look hard for a cure. In life's great spelling bee, it's easier to spell "curse" than "cure," because it's someone else's "s" that gets stuck in the middle of it all.

Logical rigor has never been a strong point among Cubs Curse cultists. Fanatics who blame the Billy Goat Curse for the lack of a World Series crown since 1945 never seem to consider the fact that the Cubs had failed to win a World Championship during the 37 years immediately *preceding* 1945 as well. Those 37 long seasons leading up to the goat incident lay every bit as devoid of Series wins as the decades After Goat (A.G.). They also featured their share of bizarre occurrences that contributed to Chicago defeats. Let's examine just a couple of notorious pre-curse examples.

In the 1929 Fall Classic, the Cubs faced the Philadelphia Athletics, piloted by the legendary manager Connie Mack. The A's had a splendid team filled with stars like Al Simmons, Jimmie Foxx, and Mickey Cochrane; but their manager set the tone right from the start, as great leaders tend to do.

Mr. Mack shocked the Cubs in Game One by choosing his seventh-best pitcher, Howard Ehmke, for the crucial Series-opening assignment. Despite only winning seven games all season, Ehmke started the key first game instead of such illustrious teammates as Lefty Grove (20 wins that season and a future Hall of Famer), George Earnshaw (24 wins), Rube Walberg (18 wins), and others.

Mack had secretly arranged for Ehmke to observe the Cubs in action at length prior to the World Series, so he would be ready to face them. Armed with his personal scouting information, Ehmke defied the odds-makers by defeating the bewildered Cubs and their excellent pitchers Charlie Root and Guy Bush by the final score of 3-1. Cubs sluggers such as Rogers Hornsby, Hack Wilson, Riggs Stephenson, and Kiki Cuyler were unable to solve the aging Ehmke's deliveries, to the astonishment of the Cubs and almost everyone in baseball. The 35-year-old mediocrity actually set a World Series record at the time by striking out 13 batters in the mighty Cubs lineup.

Then a few days later, with the A's ahead of the Cubs two games to one, Game Four's foul magic proved equal to any hex spawned by the most malevolent goat or cat. On Oct. 12, 1929, the Cubs held an immense 8-0 lead as the game entered the bottom of the 7th inning. In that most-unlucky

7th, the Athletics tallied an astonishing 10 runs, three of which scored on a devastating miscue (officially ruled an inside-the-park-homer) by the Cubs' star outfielder Hack Wilson.

To this day, the blown eight-run advantage remains the largest lead ever overcome in any World Series game; and it all happened during one unbelievable inning. Philadelphia won that game 10-8 and went on to capture the World Championship in the very next game. The Cubs led 2-0 behind ace pitcher and 22-game winner Pat Malone with just two outs to go in the last of the 9th inning; but the A's rallied yet again. Their bats suddenly came to life against Malone as they scored three runs in the 9th to win Game Five and with it the World Championship. Curses anyone?

Here's one more pre-curse example. The 1932 World Series against the powerful New York Yankees was unlikely to go Chicago's way from the outset, given that the Yanks boasted one of the greatest lineups of all time, coupled with excellent pitching led by Lefty Gomez. Their famous "Murderers' Row" included such future Hall of Famers as Earle Combs, Tony Lazzeri, Bill Dickey, plus a couple of guys by the name of Babe Ruth and Lou Gehrig. The predictable script was going according to form as the Yankees beat the Cubs in both of the first two games by scores of 12-6 and 5-2. However, Game Three in Wrigley Field on Oct. 1 included an event so strange and controversial it could only have befallen the Cubs. It remains one of the most debated and most disputed events in baseball history.

The score was tied 4-4 with one out in the 5th, when Babe Ruth came up to bat against ace pitcher Charlie Root. Ruth had already slugged a three-run homer against Root in the 1st inning. With a count of two strikes and two balls, the partisan Cubs crowd yelled vicious abuse at Ruth, and the Cubs players did the same. With the din at ear-splitting volume, Ruth reacted by pointing (depending on which version you believe) either at the center-field stands or at the pitcher. On the very next pitch from Root, the Babe crushed a mammoth, towering drive far over the center-field wall to put the Yankees ahead.

The disappearing baseball suddenly sucked all the air and noise out of Wrigley Field. As Ruth rounded the bases, he chuckled to himself, "You lucky bum! You lucky, lucky bum!" Some witnesses thought that Ruth had intended to show Root that he still had one strike left. Others, including Yankee first baseman Lou Gehrig (who was waiting nearby on-deck at the time) believed that Ruth truly had "called his shot" with the gesture, predicting and then immediately delivering a home run under incredible circumstances.

In any event, Gehrig added two home runs of his own, and the Yankees topped the Cubs in Game Three, 7-5. They completed their four-game sweep of the shell-shocked Cubs the next day, 13-6, without a goat or black cat in sight. And by all accounts, Steve Bartman would not be born for another 45 years. So who could the Cubs blame for their astounding misfortune? We have suggested the dreadful Tunguska meteor strike of 1908. At least that theory has the virtue of attributing the curse to an event that preceded it. Or maybe it was the baseball gods who conspired to pit the Chicagoans against one of the finest teams ever assembled.

Blame of any type is a genuine curse, a giant step in the loser's direction. It is worse than wasted effort, because it spends energy on accusing people and things of causing our difficulties, when instead we should be working on changing what we have in our power to change—our own attitude and behavior. We might feel better if we complain about the bad beatings we endured so unjustly because of malevolent forces beyond our control. Sympathy might flow to those who are innocently hurt, after all. And it is much easier to carp about bad luck and curses than to admit our mistakes and take corrective action. It is entirely ineffective at reducing the probability of future such mishaps, but at least it is easy on our ego and easy on our muscles. Why force ourselves to confront our failings and expend energy on correcting our deficiencies when we can so effortlessly indict Mother Nature, society, the system, and indeed A.B.O. (anything but ourselves).

Blame goes from counterproductive to cancerous when we use it to stigmatize our teammates and managers. Like parasites, we devour the essence we live in when we try to shift responsibility to other people in our organization. Even if these co-workers do legitimately deserve some reproach for their errors and lackadaisical effort, good leaders will strive to build a team approach to winning and a team approach to learning from losing.

No one person is solely responsible for triumphs or tragedies in any organization, and any attempt to make someone the scapegoat will unfairly divert all negative attention to just one target. Such infantile behavior splinters team cohesion, opening deep gashes that may never heal. Instead of unifying everyone toward a common goal of mutual support and improvement, internal blame games provoke civil wars. Who can trust a colleague when they have turned on their own friends? Who can commit to an organization that tolerates infighting and eating its young? Who can be loyal to a leader who permits disloyalty and self-consuming buck passing?

It is almost as bad to succumb to a culture of defeatism. Like the Cubs' infamous "curse" which allegedly has used supernatural powers to deny them victory for decades, some organizations allow a demoralized sense of gloom and hopelessness to pervade the spirit of their enterprise. The attitude is one of resignation and fatalism, as if failure were a foreordained destiny for everyone unfortunate enough to fall within the organization's reach. Large, old bureaucracies sometimes acquire this affliction, accumulated over many years of fetid performance, broken systems of rewards/accountability, impenetrable administrivia, and unclear vision.

The leader's vision must always correspond to the problem. When a curse mentality is allowed to take root, people begin expecting disaster—not so they can effectively counter it, but as an inevitable conclusion to whatever promising beginning they might muster. This breeds an attitude of insecurity and self-doubt, a lack of confidence that finds people always looking over their shoulders for the next catastrophe. Instead of healthy self-assurance bred of competence, we find tentativeness, anxiety, passivity, over-cautiousness, despair, and fear. In any organization, pain is a part of life, but misery is an option. Good leaders can go a long way toward eliminating both pain and misery.

From a rational standpoint, no one should believe in curses this many centuries removed from the Dark Ages. But belief in foul and mysterious magical opposition can still fester when leaders fail to inculcate a firm spirit of unity, continuous improvement, acceptance of and learning from our mistakes, and a top-to-bottom attitude of confident achievement.

If people don't have faith in their own abilities and are ever fearful of impending doom, they will be more prone to folding under pressure. They will make mistakes at key moments. They will forget all they know about winning because they are so haunted by the ghosts of past failures. When faced with assured, relaxed, exuberant, professional competition, the curse-ridden team will make foolish errors, blow mishaps out of proportion, refrain from capitalizing on positive opportunities, and allow the other side to take control. When the worst does happen, these losers can comfort themselves with the delusion that it had nothing to do with their own shortcomings. It was the curse, the system, the society, the culture, and the cluster of bad luck that always dogs the innocent.

The Cubs have long blamed their "Billy Goat" Curse (literally a scapegoat) for their record-breaking string of disappointments, just as the Boston Red Sox once pinned their losses on the "Curse of the Bambino," and the Chicago White Sox deflected responsibility for their failures onto the "Black Sox" curse. The Red Sox finally broke their "curse" with a World Championship in 2004, and the White Sox followed suit in 2005. But the Cubs still cling tenaciously to their permanent, perpetual excuse generator.

Beyond the sports world, similar curses abound, disguised as such responsibility-evading phenomena as racism, poverty, language barriers, sexism, political disadvantage, religious discrimination, affirmative action, reverse discrimination, and many related beasts. All of these are real concerns, and all of them can be formidable barriers to individual and collective success…but all of them only become insurmountable obstacles if we ourselves elevate them to that status by preemptively declaring defeat.

When we surrender, we might feel a sense of relief, because we no longer expect much from ourselves, and we beg others to concur. If we foster a cocoon of low expectations, we insulate ourselves from disappointment, and we can attribute our paucity of achievements to external injustices—not our own faults. This absence of personal accountability can be addictive. It feels safe and comfortable to be babied, to have everyone trying to take care of us no matter—or because of—how little we produce. But dependency and complacency lead only to more of the same.

Genuine success only exists beyond the limits of the comfort zone, in the realm where our actions have consequences, good and bad. Success becomes possible only when we accept that there are no true curses other than those we embrace as our own crutches. When we believe in the fiction these curses embody, we bring the curses to life, like a perversely twisted and malign Tinker Bell animated by our misguided faith.

In a way, everyone who indulges in the blame game also gives in to the medieval curse mentality. When we refuse to accept responsibility for our own missteps, we implicitly acknowledge the existence of a curse that cruelly deprives us of the rewards that are rightfully ours. We admit to ourselves and to others that we are impotent in the face of unseen malevolent powers. We take ownership of our own powerlessness, and embrace it, as a permanent badge of futility.

How else should we interpret the attitude that we are helplessly at the mercy of everyone and everything, that our best efforts are wasted in any contest with such an unjust world? People loaded down with this accursed curse baggage are not going to look to themselves for a way to better results, because all such efforts are in vain and predestined to fail. Their self-authored script is structured around the premise that the system stinks, and there's nothing we can do about it. This "stinking thinking" mindset is an ideal breeding ground for persistent failure. It abandons the only realistic path to betterment—our determination, our hard work, our positive attitude, our tenacity—and surrenders to the role of eternal victim.

Life can very easily seem unfair to anyone who allows such thoughts to gain a foothold in his or her brain. The Cubs and their fans have succumbed to feelings of persecution, unfairness, and curse-rehearsing many times, and why not? Fine teams such as the Cubs of 2007 and 2008 were meticulously assembled, piece by piece, over a period of several years. Both years, the teams worked hard all during spring training and the long, exhausting, 162-game regular season to win the National League Central Division championship, coming in first after all those months of determined, day-by-day persistence. The 2008 Cubs actually achieved the best regular-season record in the entire National League, winning 97 games (the most by a Cubs team in 63 years, since their last World Series appearance in 1945) and remaining in first place continuously from May all the way through to season's end. They were widely praised as the top team in the league, if not all of baseball, and some were bold enough to predict the long-awaited Cubs World Series championship.

Then, in both 2007 and 2008, after so much prolonged effort and such impressive accomplishments, it all ended in the very first round of the playoffs—a best three-out-of-five-games Division Series where the first team to win three games advances to the next round, and the loser goes home until next year. At least the Cubs made it end quickly and didn't prolong the agony. In both the 2007 and 2008 Division Series, the Cubs were swept away in three straight games, unable to scratch out even a single win. The Cubs had won the marathon, but lost the sprint, two years in a row.

The Cubs' sickening unbroken string of eight consecutive postseason losses began in 2003 with the devastating "Bartman incident." That stunning, high-visibility setback didn't confine its damage just to the 2003 team.

It turned out to have thoroughly spread its deadly poison throughout their next two playoff series as well, repeatedly leaving the team and their fans in shock. The players that had done so well throughout the lengthy regular season challenges suddenly froze up under the magnified short-term stress of the playoff spotlight, perhaps in fear of another Bartman-type fiasco.

Let's brace ourselves and cite just a few specific examples from 2008, where the countless regular-season thrills made the sudden collapse in the playoffs all the more bitter.

Star pitcher Ryan Dempster, who had scarcely lost a game in Wrigley Field all year (winning 14 games against just three defeats), suddenly lost control in Game One of the 2008 Division Series. The normally dominant control pitcher went wild and issued seven walks en route to a demoralizing 7-2 loss to the Los Angeles Dodgers in front of a packed house of horrified Cubs fans. The next night, in Game Two, every one of the Cubs' ordinarily sure-handed infielders committed fielding errors, and the Cubs were buried alive under an avalanche of unearned runs, 10-3. Finally, the Cubs were almost completely shut down in Los Angeles in Game Three, plating just one run in a lifeless 3-1 defeat that finished off another quick exit from the postseason. In dropping all three games, the 2008 Cubs could only tally a measly total of six runs, despite leading the league in runs scored for the year. In both 2007 and 2008, once the playoffs began, their entire lineup of powerful, talented hitters abruptly went on strike, or strikeout, and the tension-strangled Cubs could barely manage to score at all.

It all seemed terribly unjust to the mighty 2008 Cubs and their disillusioned fans, and with good reason. Of course it can feel unfair and unrepresentative to have a whole long season—162 games—of sustained excellence under conditions of prolonged and intense competition negated by one short rough spot. But unfair or not, it is a fact of life. It can happen to the best of teams, and it has, many times. Especially, needless to say, to the Cubs. But if this setup is unfair and arbitrary in some sense, it is nonetheless the same system that applies equally across the board to everyone in the game; and every participant in major league baseball knew about it all along.

Is it any different from the situation in which a leader spearheads her business to superlative productivity, consistently and reliably, for months or years without interruption, only to have all that success jeopardized by a single brief inspection or site visit from an outside evaluator? Is it fundamentally in a separate category from the plight of a hard-working student who spends many years in school, from kindergarten through high school, college, or graduate school, diligently studying and preparing every day, and then finds his future dangling from his performance on just one short, pressure-laden examination (such as the SAT, MCAT, GMAT, LSAT, GRE, bar exam, or medical boards)?

Anything can happen during one quick snapshot, as our family photo albums prove. A bad day, or a tough clump of days, can ruin years and even decades of first-rate work, just as an instant's unfortunate facial expression or a one-day pimple while someone is taking pictures for a school year-book can forevermore change the way our classmates remember us. This is objectively unfair, in the sense that it doesn't accurately represent the long-term, big-picture reality and quality of who we are and what we do; but leaders must proactively deal with that unfairness, plan for it, and fight to overcome it.

When things go badly under all that pressure, these crushing short-term setbacks are like a hard punch in the pit of the stomach, and it is so easy to give up, lest hope once again be crushed at the end of so much protracted, dedicated, persistent work. But a Cubs Fan leader must figure out how to pick out some useful lessons from among the debris and get the team back together to begin, once again, the slow, arduous, daily toil of renewing the push toward success. When leaders instead choose to cry about unfairness and join the mournful chorus of weeping perpetual victims, their helpless and passive attitude soaks through the entire organization's affective culture...and the team continues to lose, unfairly, again and again.

One of the biggest challenges any leader faces is how to rally an organization after it has suffered a devastating setback. A major loss is always hard to overcome, but the worst type is the one we've just been discussing, in which months or years of determined, dedicated work are undone in a flash. How can Sisyphus summon up the will to trudge all the way back down the hill and, yet again, resume the arduous labor of pushing that heavy boulder toward the top one more time? How can the highly touted Cubs of 2008, lugging the weight of a full century of losing, emerge from the heartbreak of a second consecutive first-round playoff defeat? How can this disappointed and disappointing team resolve to put the loss behind them and take up the challenge of another grueling six months of exhausting regular-season competition before they even have another chance at the playoffs?

When you're all at once back where you started from so long ago at square one, life can seem like one big, cruel game of "Chutes and Ladders," and the long, snaking road to the top can appear to stretch on past infinity. That excruciating view from the absolute bottom makes it much more tempting to give up than to give chase.

Actually, such a crushing, abrupt loss finds no solution in either giving up or giving chase...at least if by "giving chase" we mean that we abandon our usual discipline and flail away recklessly. The correct decision when we suffer a wrenching, decimating setback is nowhere near as interesting as the extremes of a panicked retreat or a heroic, suicidal frontal counterattack. In fact, a leader should choose neither, and instead head straight for the boring middle ground. It is wildly unrealistic to expect to recoup huge losses—which required long periods of persistent effort to gain—as quickly as they were taken from us. It's always quicker and easier to destroy than to build. Whether we quit trying altogether, or forget all our fundamentals in a frantic vengeance-drunk frenzy, we only compound our defeat and guarantee its permanence.

The proper option is not exciting, bold, thrilling, breathtakingly aggressive, or stunningly rapid in its rewards. Rather, it involves nothing flashier than keeping the team from succumbing to emotional extremes, and helping everyone remember how *the team* amassed all those gains in the first place, step by measured step.

The leader has to stay in control and under control, and help the team resist the instinctive impulse to run in either direction, whether fleeing in disarray or charging blindly ahead. A sudden bad beat or hard fall down a steep chute is the worst possible time for running. The leader must get everyone to focus once more on the basics—the core competencies that, in the long haul, enable the organization to rebuild. No matter how much it hurts to lose what it took so long to achieve, it is absolutely crucial not to dwell on the devastation's magnitude, the downturn's unfairness, or the vastness and seeming impossibility of the rebuilding task ahead. The leader needs to get the team's attention off of those dead ends and pointed in the only direction that has any possibility of recovery. Beginning with the leader, everyone must walk, not run, onto the long, slow path back toward the goal.

Most of us can remember times when we've had to struggle through a similar challenge in our own lives. A poker player must rebound from a bad beat that costs him, in a single hand, most of his carefully acquired stack of chips. He can't allow himself to get angry or disheartened and go "on tilt." Rather, he has to somehow keep focused and calm, maintain his composure and perspective, and return to the slow, incremental, patient, persistent task of building his stack back up.

Likewise, the leader of any organization has the same type of problem when her unit is devastated by a disastrous fire, flood, hurricane, or earthquake, or by a poor performance on an outside evaluation, or by a sudden corporate decision to downsize, or by a negative news media report on the organization's problems. The leader needs to regain the initiative and inspire her team to get back to the rock-solid daily fundamentals—the routine, steady pursuit of basic, normal, bite-sized chunks of excellence that might eventually rebuild the unit and recoup the losses. At least the calm, long-view approach has a much better chance of someday making up all that lost ground than a sudden, frenetic spasm of "Hail Mary" desperation moves.

Here's the reason this is so difficult, and the reason the Cubs and many of us have so often failed to rebound from sudden bitter disappointment: It's human nature to react negatively to such negative experiences. What could be more natural when life deals us a bad beat than to despair and/or get mad, and to want either to run away or to get even in a hurry? When we feel wronged and hurt by bad luck or prejudice or unfair assessment of our work, our first reaction is usually not to dust ourselves off and patiently begin the laborious, gradual, seemingly endless process of doggedly repairing the damage. We want to lash out, retaliate, give up, get hyperaggressive, throw a pity party, or sue someone—whatever means are necessary to ease our pain.

It takes a lot of maturity and equanimity to say to ourselves, "That's poker!" or "That's life!" and get right back to work doing all the countless little detailed tasks, every day, that can in the long (and we do mean long) run bring success. As leaders, it is only by controlling our reactions to that bad beat that we can exert positive influence on our organization's affective culture. Only in this way can we maintain any real chance of helping everyone eventually climb back out of the hole into which we've suddenly fallen.

The affective culture of any group of people—whether a professional sports team, a faculty, a governmental department, a small business, a multinational corporation, or an entire nation—is simultaneously one of the most vital and one of the most maddeningly elusive features with which a leader must work. Affective culture is the realm of the emotional, where the visceral, feelings-packed, gut-level core of our people dominates. Here is foreign turf for leaders who operate strictly on the level of logic, rationality, and cold, crisp reasoning. But just as people without feelings are robots, a team emptied of its affective elements is a machine. And robots or machines can do many things, and do them very well, but they are hopeless when circumstances demand inspiration, breakthrough-grade improvisation, motivational self-sacrifice, and off-the-charts devotion to a cause.

The Cubs have developed a negative affective culture over the span of their many decades of failure and disappointment. They never did this intentionally, of course. They have always had at least a sprinkling of talented, enthusiastic players, knowledgeable managers, and earnest front-office executives. At times, they've had entire teams filled with solid-to-excellent performers, and they have acquitted themselves admirably over the long haul of full 162-game regular seasons, even entering the postseason as statistical favorites to win it all. But the curse mentality has gradually put down deep and far-reaching roots, and the habit of losing has had so many years to metastasize its way into the heart of the culture. These potent producers of impotence could have been preemptively headed off with the right leadership at the right time, but instead of rescuing the team with effective leadership, the Cubs long ago drifted into an affective swamp of fatalism.

It's an insidious process by which a healthy organization gets parasitized by invisible, often slow-acting agents of complacency, apathy, pessimism, mutual distrust, lack of buy-in, lethargy, hopelessness, and inertia. It took numerous seasons of varying types of losses for the Cubs to slip from great to good, from good to mediocre, and from mediocre to atrocious. The same is undoubtedly true for most if not all agglomerations of human beings who have learned the losing lessons at the primitive, affective level. Such painstakingly protracted and pain-inflicting tutorials on losing leave marks of such degree and down-to-the-bone depth that only the strongest remedies have any hope of working. When the affective culture is sick, it takes a lot more than a couple of leadership aspirins to get to the real trouble.

It's easy to tell when a sports team is losing, because there's always someone officially keeping score, and the results are widely available. Losses in other types of organizations can be much trickier to detect, and the reasons are often related to the problems that are themselves causing the unsatisfactory results. Groups that don't keep track of what they are doing, or are lax about measuring performance (individually and collectively), or fail to communicate performance assessment data, or attach no real consequences to poor output, are likely to develop a sick affective culture. This is in part precisely because no one seems to be watching or caring much about what is being done.

In such contexts, people understandably slip into a losing attitude due to a pervasive feeling that nothing they do matters to anyone. Why work hard or strive to be creative when neither your leaders nor your colleagues are paying attention or behaving as if it made any difference to them? Human beings have an innate need to create and produce; but that instinct must be nurtured and supported, or it will gradually wither and dry up. In a who-cares affective culture, even the brightest self-starter may eventually decide to shut down, or move to more fertile territory.

Losses in these non-sports aggregations won't tend to be as dramatic or obvious as the Cubs' very public failings. If external pressures such as competition and the need to make a profit are weak or absent, the whole cluster can slouch along from year to year, never leaving the comfort of the accursed rut.

What cliché would fit life in this type of situation? Here are a few candidates (and for those playing the home version of this game, you can try to come up with some others): treading water, mailing it in, asleep at the switch, retired on the job, good enough for government work, don't rock the boat, and wake me when it's quitting time.

People in such losing organizations tend to have their hearts and minds set on drawing their paychecks and minimizing their personal discomfort and inconvenience while trapped at what passes for the workplace. They probably have never suffered a catastrophic or high-profile loss worthy of a Cubs-like scapegoat curse, but they are cursed nonetheless with an affective culture where poor performance is tolerated, apathy is the norm, and the status quo is as far as anyone wants to go.

When we give in to the A.B.O. philosophy, we cut out our heart. We throw away personal responsibility for our life, our status, our circumstances, and our career. We abdicate accountability for everything that happens to us, and pin the blame on the scapegoat. If we can convince ourselves that we play no part in engineering our failures, we guarantee that we will do nothing to help ourselves. And that, in turn, guarantees that we will continue to be victimized by all those old familiar curses. Welcome to scapegoat central.

The only effective escape route from this labyrinth of lamentations is the one painstakingly carved out every day by a game-changing, blame-blamming leader. A leader can positively affect a sick affective culture most dramatically and permanently by exemplifying the Trumanesque principle "The buck stops here." Team members will take notice that something different is happening when they begin to see their leader consistently taking personal responsibility for poor results and substandard efforts, rather than yelling at the employees, whining about unfair competition, or moaning about bad luck. They will pay attention when their leader refuses to hear their own bad-beat complaints and buck-passing excuses. They will catch on when their leader regularly demonstrates firm commitment to the idea that a person's "I will" is more important than their I.Q. When the leader, day after day, without exception, publicly and privately values commitment, dedication, best effort, and acceptance of responsibility, then members of the organization will eventually get the message. On a winning team, when bad things happen to good people, blaming anyone but ourselves has no place on anyone's to-do list.

7th Inning Discussion Questions

1. To what extent are bad luck or "curses" genuine phenomena that individuals and teams must learn to handle?

2. Do you think particular sets of conditions tend to generate belief in mysterious negative forces such as bad luck or "curses?"

3. How can a leader help his or her people overcome a mindset that reinforces belief in persistent bad luck or inevitable defeat?

4. Are certain types of organizations more vulnerable than others to the "blame game?" What factors foster the tendency to refuse responsibility and to transfer blame to others? How can a leader move people to accept responsibility for their own actions and reactions? Is today's culture in general a help or a hindrance? Why?

5. Have you ever known a leader who refused to accept blame and who attempted to transfer accountability to others when things went wrong? What effect did this have on the organization?

6. Define, in your own words, "luck." How can a leader exert any influence on luck? What if any role has luck played in your life?

7. How, if at all, should a leader deal with luck and people's belief in it/reactions to it?

8. How do you usually respond to a "bad beat?" How do your team members react in similar situations?

9. What is the impact on your organization from your mode of handling "unfair" adversity?

10. In what respects is it fair or unfair to judge a leader or an organization on the basis of a brief inspection or externally-imposed test? How can a leader incorporate the reality of such short-term, artificial challenges into his or her plans and preparations?

8th Inning
Treasure the Past, but Don't Bury the Future in It

It is beyond dispute that the Chicago Cubs have a grand and glorious past, adorned with traditions and storybook heroes. The very ballpark in which they play, Wrigley Field, has long given new and special meaning to "Ivy League," with the park's legendary, verdantly living outfield walls so tantalizingly close they invited hitters to swing for the fences. Since 1914 this green cathedral of baseball has exuded history. Within the picture-perfect frame of its "friendly confines" vine-yard, generations of Hall of Famers have achieved near-mythical feats of greatness. Decade upon decade, splendid teams and fabled stars have amassed a past worthy of reverent admiration. Indeed, with a past like that, who needs a present, or a future?

The Cubs were the last team in the major leagues to install and use the lights necessary to play games at night. Not until 1988 did night baseball arrive at Wrigley Field, and the event was tantamount to sacrilege in the minds of many tradition-loving Cubs fans. Some critics have suggested that the long delay in adding lights had more to do with penny-pinching than tradition-hugging on the part of the team owners. There may be elements of truth to both views, as well as the notion that the team desired to be good neighbors, saving nearby residents from suffering thousands of rowdy passersby while they were trying to sleep. Whatever the primary reason, the lightless spotlight shone on Wrigley Field for many years, magnifying the no-night-baseball issue far beyond its true importance, and distracting attention from matters much more directly connected to winning.

The lights-out crusade became emblematic of the Cubs emphasis, or over-emphasis, on their glorious past and their gorgeous, venerable, green cathedral of baseball. It seemed to numerous fans that bringing night baseball to traditionalism's shrine at the corner of Addison and Sheffield would be tantamount to sacrilege, an act of utter disregard for long-established values. The prospect of increased attendance, better television ratings, more favorable playing conditions for tired players in the heat of summer, and improved relations with the league's other teams could not dislodge the early-to-bed army from its Maginot Line of stasis. Only after an astonishingly protracted debate and bitter controversy did baseballs finally fly by night in Wrigley Field; and in the meantime, additional decades full of flag-free Octobers piled up in Chicago.

Wrigley Field itself has begun falling apart during the last few years, with large chunks of material crashing down from the upper deck onto the seats below. These structural problems, as with the night-baseball dust-up, symbolize the team's reluctance to make bold changes on and off the field as well. The Cubs have become and remained a national icon without undergoing radical change, and many believe that its stature would be diminished by succumbing to shifting trends. Thus, evolution proceeds very slowly at best in and around Wrigley Field. Even in the era of high-priced free agents and astronomical player salaries, the Cubs have often spent their big-market money like a small-market team. When the team can make a huge profit without doing what it takes to invest in an actual championship, why mess with success, or the lack thereof?

Of course, much is good, even wondrous, about the Cubs' heritage, from its beautiful stadium to its long list of heroes. But it may be that this legacy comes with strings attached. Indeed, this leadership lesson is tied to another—the importance of not growing inured to persistent failure. A powerfully seductive appeal exists to stand pat when substantial rewards and awards flow unabated regardless of actual successful results. Along with that, an almost irresistible impulse urges us to stay the course when the status quo enjoys enormous popular support; and it's propped up by traditions from a glorious past.

When customers, onlookers, and upper-level executives actively promote historic grandeur and oppose the stupendous heresy of modernization, the easiest and safest plan of action seems to be this: Take as little action as possible. History cannot dictate the future, but it can enhance the decision-making process for better days ahead. The Cubs and Cubs Fan leaders should see the glorious past as a challenge to do better things in the future.

This penchant for nostalgia, savoring memories from a more won-drous yesterday, afflicts individuals and organizations at all levels. Even entire nations can buy into complacent inertia, content to coast on former achievements and live off of long-ago successes.

At work, no one wants to fire the elder statesman of the company, even if he has not produced any meaningful achievements for years. Sentimentality and shared memories insulate the hanger-on, especially when he was once a star performer. It can seem heartless to insist on current productivity from a venerable old veteran who once may have served as a mentor and protector to many people now in top responsible positions. Few want to be accused of ingratitude along the lines of "What have you done for me lately?" So it is more comfortable simply to let things slide, and to continue to slide.

Don't read the following joke if you've already heard it more than 43 times. How many psychiatrists does it take to change a light bulb? The answer is simple. Only one, but it is very expensive, takes a long time, and the light bulb must want to change.

However, the legendary light bulb notwithstanding, it is a myth that change takes a long time. The Cubs may not always get it, but it's true. Change can happen very quickly at times, while at other times it crawls with imperceptible, glacier-like slowness. This is true of all types of evolution, whether good or bad. A major function of leaders is to maximize the former and minimize the latter. Lou Piniella did this as the Cubs' new manager in 2007 when he took them from last place to first in their division.

Positive change—the kind that we proactively cause, rather than the kind that falls on top of us by default—requires the right strategy. We need a system, including a workable and institutionally internalized process, to bring about the good-news change and identify/dodge the car-crash kind. An effective leader engineers useful change. Without that leader, change will inevitably find us anyway, even as we sit still; and that variety of acci-dental change will usually not be welcome.

Here's a major lesson Cubs fans should derive from highly successful leaders: Only in change is there security. Change is necessary for ongoing improvement, because the context, the environment within which we function, is continually evolving. We cannot expect the same old methods to apply equally well to the new and shifting conditions.

When implemented properly, change is life-giving. It helps us grow into someone or something greater. Those who fail to adapt will face an unenviable future like a hopelessly out-of-date Rip Van Winkle at last awakening from a prolonged slumber. Clearly, we as leaders will not be able to control everything that happens to us. But we are in complete control of how we respond to what happens; and we can also proactively influence events to a significant extent if we are equipped with accurate information, and if we affirmatively and actively seek untapped ways to channel the future in a positive direction.

This is the age of instability. It can be an uncomfortable time for people who long for things to remain as they are, familiar, well-understood, and routine. With continual change a given, a leader must resolve to put change to work, to squeeze a harness around it and ride it toward the right horizon. More than ever before, the 21st-Century leader must effectively engage and manage change. The best way to predict the future is to invent it, but we can't do that by mechanically applying any formula from a self-help book, and there are no do-it-yourself kits for this. No matter what neologisms we create to describe our methods, and irrespective of how many charts and four-part-process lists we concoct to conjure the illusion of quantifiable precision, we still glimpse the future, if at all, through a glass, darkly. But we can look at what we need now, and what we will need two years from now, and set purposefully about making it happen.

Let's devote significant amounts of time on a regular basis to meeting with our people at all levels, brainstorming ideas for dealing with the years to come. We will find ready confirmation of our suspicion that we don't know all the answers, nor do we possess a monopoly on all the good questions.

We will also find that action works like a powerful medicine to relieve feelings of fear, helplessness, anger, and uncertainty, because we become no longer just passive passengers on a runaway train, but rather engineers with influence over our journey. Instead of changing with the times, we must make a habit of changing just a little ahead of the times, and doing what we can to nudge change in the optimal direction.

Because the future is now, we should start this process now. If we do not, we will find ourselves running through the forest of common sense without seeing a single tree, or blind to a big brick wall because of all the vines in the way.

Many leaders find this brand of forward-looking creativity and long-range planning a decidedly uncomfortable fit. People tend to feel that any attempt to gauge the need for modifications—to anticipate troubles ahead and make corrections, and to ferret out hidden time-bombs ticking within their midst—is an accusation against current leadership. They fear it's an admission that the leader has been imperfect, even a failure. An insecure leader can feel vulnerable, and may in fact *be* vulnerable, in a highly competitive environment...but it does no good to retreat inside a shell and pretend all is well. The sense of security conjured up by raising the drawbridge and going into siege mode won't last long. Eventually inaction and complacency will allow the organization to be overcome by unopposed and unforeseen threats. Acting as if there is no need for self-examination and periodic change does not transform fantasy into reality. It is delusional and dangerous, symptomatic of leadership so tentative and timid that it sees any suggestion of adjustment as an insult and a challenge to authority.

If you are a leader who has made mistakes, here is one of the most powerful and most difficult courses of action for you to take: Confront the mistakes directly, accept responsibility, and join in an authentic quest to learn from those mistakes. As master teacher Marva Collins tells her students, "Don't be afraid to make a mistake. If you can't make a mistake, you can't make anything."

Leaders with eggshell egos recoil at the first hint of acknowledging their mistakes; but if they would remove their blinders they would see that everyone but them already is well aware of their errors. We can't hide our mistakes by masquerading as infallible. The charade of flawlessness only proves we are fools, and fools fool no one but themselves. The pose of infallibility undermines our stature among our people, who see at the helm only a pathetic, deluded fraud and coward, unwilling or unable to admit mistakes. It's a poison pill of pretense. Worse, putting on airs of inerrancy robs us and our organization of the opportunity to turn our missteps into stepping stones: useful data points in the unending process of advancement by trial and error.

To remain competitive in a rolling environment, leaders must be willing, even eager, to acknowledge room for positive change and continuous re-evaluation, beginning at the top. This doesn't require leaders to make a dramatic, tearful, lip-biting confession that they have failed terribly and let everyone down. Rather leaders can start with themselves and demonstrate that everyone at all levels can do better, making adjustments to stay ahead of ever-evolving challenges.

A refusal to tolerate self-satisfied, stand-pat complacency means a serious commitment to perpetual improvement in everyone, with utterly zero exceptions. That realistic and honest attitude is evidence of strength, not weakness, and is absolutely essential if the leader is to steer clear of devastation. Even current success is not necessarily an excuse for remaining static, because what has worked before may not continue to work as circumstances reshuffle. Often, to effect change implies making waves, and if you don't make waves, you'll drown.

Those who remain satisfied with that which isn't broken can be disappointed one day, finding that unbroken processes, products, and plans have nevertheless become obsolete, and thus worthless. Competitors are forever out there working indefatigably to invent ways to gain an advantage. Customers are always alert for faster, cheaper, and better alternatives. Society itself is in constant motion, with fashions and passions shifting in often surprising ways.

So leaders must not assume that staying the course is the only plan that validates the excellence of their own leadership skills. After all, full speed ahead only works as long as someone is at the helm watching for hidden icebergs. Failure doesn't come from recognizing that icebergs are present and that they could sink the ship, but from pretending that everything is perfect and no change of course is ever necessary...and paying no heed to those nasty storm clouds and chunks of ice in the distance.

Management by mistake, or rather management by modifications from mistakes, is unsettlingly messy in its implementation and unsteady in its progress. It is painful to admit mistakes, and humbling to ask for suggestions from people at the lowest pay grade. Learning, teaching, strategic planning, and mentoring require plenty of time, persistent effort, and an abundance of patience. Harvests almost always come about slowly, and don't tend to adhere closely to anyone's advance expectations or a preprinted timetable.

For managers who crave the quick and easy fix of liposuction leadership, it can be very disconcerting to realize how long and tortuous the process of Cubs Fan leadership is, and how many zigs, let alone how many zags, point the nonlinear way in the general direction of improvement. It isn't as elegant and beautiful as the shiny models advocated by so many theoreticians in their bestsellers; but when everything is hanging over a cliff, solid leadership has the virtue of producing results in the real world while papier-mâché paradigms are paralyzed. Except in the musical play "How to Succeed in Business Without Really Trying" we seldom find a how-to book that actually does provide a working, near-effortless blueprint for predictable and facile success. But the principles under consideration in this book present authentic, if sweaty, elements of sound leadership.

People have a natural tendency to avoid the unknown, clinging to the familiar even when the past isn't so glorious. The way things have always been done is the only way most people in the organization have ever known. They learned it as novices, and saw it routinized and standardized through many years of repetition until it has become habitual and reflexive. Everyone is within his or her comfort zone with the long-standing standard operating procedure. There is little or no uncharted territory, and few if any unpleasant surprises, because so many people have stuck with the same plan for so long. Keeping it up is as effortless and cozy as slipping on our favorite old sweater yet again, as television's Mr. Rogers did, every episode, decade after decade. Everything is just as we expected, just as it has always been, and we feel at home, comfortable and protected.

Those aren't inherently negative emotions. When warranted by reality, they are among the benefits of a job well done…but only temporary, not unending benefits. It's fine to encourage our employees to celebrate an achievement and to take an occasional well-deserved vacation. Those delectable carrots are part of the bumper crop we collect when we obey the law of the harvest. But when we tolerate the revelry and respite, lingering on beyond the normal "cool of the evening" that follows a difficult challenge, we risk falling into the Cubs' tradition prison. Beneficial relaxing can ossify into detrimental resting on our laurels. All it takes is a leader willing to stay on cruise control a little too long. A little too long is just a step removed from a little bit longer, and then a little longer still. And why not, when no one is complaining and everyone looks happy?

This is one of those situations that separate good leaders from bad ones, because it demands a fine sense of balance. Leaders must negotiate a course between two extremes. On one side hovers the danger of driving our people too hard, relentlessly applying the pressure, never letting up for a moment's respite no matter how much the organization achieves. On the other side, the danger of complacency lies on a comfy, overstuffed bed of wilted laurels. Certainly, more people within the organization will be pleased with the latter approach, because it makes life much sweeter for them, at least while it lasts. And if there is sufficient approval from higher-ups, and a supportive customer/fan base, the leader has even more incentive to let things be—to leave things unfixed as long as they seem not to be flat-out broken.

This is why the tradition prison is the more common, and ultimately more destructive, error leaders make when they fail to maintain organizational equilibrium. Leaders, like everyone else, love to hear the cheers of the crowd and lots of praise from workers and supervisors, so they tend to favor the kinder, gentler, easier option.

Why haven't the Cubs learned enough from their history to bring back the best of it? Remember, way back when the World Series was brand new? The Cubs were in three consecutive World Series, winning the last two of them (in 1907 and 1908). Although those teams are best remembered for their double-play combination (Tinker to Evers to Chance) because of a poem that made it famous (Baseball's Sad Lexicon), there were other key ingredients that made them world-beaters. The renowned infield was rounded out by hard-hitting stars at third base (Harry Steinfeldt) and catcher (Johnny Kling). The outfield was filled with standouts such as Frank "Wildfire" Schulte, Jimmy Sheckard, and Jim "Rabbit" Slagle. But perhaps even more so than all of these strengths, the pitching staff was the real heart of these superb teams. The Cubs collection of iron-clad moundsmen included four nonstop aces: Mordecai "Three Finger" Brown, Ed Reulbach, Jack Pfeister, and Orval Overall. How effective were these pitchers? During the three full seasons from 1906 through 1908, the *highest* Earned Run Average any of them ever posted was "Big Ed" Reulbach's 1908 microscopic 2.03 runs per game. Even within the context of that low-scoring dead-ball period, the Cubs pitching stood superlative beyond belief.

Mordecai Brown was *the* ace of the Cubs' quad aces. His story is inspirational to anyone faced with tragedy, unfairness, and disadvantage. While he was a boy growing up on a farm, he dreamed of becoming a great right-handed pitcher in the major leagues. Bitter reality intruded one day when he badly injured his right hand, slipping while he was putting material into his family's feed chopper. The sharp-bladed machinery severed much of his index finger and mangled other fingers as well. He later aggravated this injury during a fall, and some of the broken bones were improperly set. As a result of these two horrible mishaps, his hand was permanently, severely damaged, earning him the unusual and somewhat inaccurate nickname "Three Finger."

But like the resourceful leader he was, Brown worked hard until he found a way to put his disfigured hand to good use. He learned to use his unique right hand to make baseballs perform tricks the likes of which no one had ever before seen. He didn't merely make lemonade from the lemons life gave him—he took it to the next level, turning a horror-movie pitching hand into a career's worth of nightmares for opposing hitters. On his way to the Hall of Fame, he achieved the following set of amazing numbers during the Cubs' three successive glory years from 1906 to 1908.

YEAR	WINS	LOSSES	E.R.A.
1906	26	6	1.04
1907	20	6	1.39
1908	29	9	1.47

He didn't stop there, either. From 1909 through 1911 he notched 27, 25, and 21 victories each year, respectively. Such spectacular pitching by Three Finger Brown and his colleagues made the Cubs almost unbeatable when combined with hermetic defense, great speed, sound fundamental skills, inspirational leadership (from player-manager Frank "The Peerless Leader" Chance) and solid hitting. Indeed, the Cubs began the 20th Century with an ideal blueprint for continued excellence. But as the members of those wonderful teams departed one by one, no one remained to ensure that the right traditions were preserved. In baseball as in life, it takes far less time to destroy a legacy than to build one.

Oblivious to their own earlier winning ways, for much of the Cubs' prolonged doldrums team leaders have emphasized homerun power and neglected pitching and defense. Their own leaders thought that long-ball power was the key to victory, and not the delicate blend of stellar pitching and across-the-board integrated excellence that brought the team so much early success.

In part this was a response to the cozy, slugger-friendly dimensions of Wrigley Field, whose nearby outfield walls seemed tailor-made for homer-happy brawlers; but it overlooked the fundamental soundness that lay at the foundation of every successful Cubs team. From the very beginning, whenever the Cubs won, it was only when they relied on much more than an unbalanced, power-pumped approach.

But it became easier and a more obvious choice to stress crowd-pleasing home runs over the subtleties of a complex, calibrated equilibrium that skillfully combined pitching, speed, solid all-around skills, versatile hitting, attention to fine details, and defense. Repeatedly the Cubs leadership sought out mid- to late-career sluggers along the lines of Ralph Kiner, Dave Kingman, George Bell, and other one-dimensional, boom-or-bust musclemen. The homer-heavy paradigm failed to win year after year; but fans love to see the fireworks, and Wrigley Field was made for the long ball. Or so the Big Bang Theory goes.

It's one thing for a leader to study the past to gather, judiciously and selectively, some practical lessons. It's quite another matter for a tradition-shackled, backward-gazing leader's fixation on the good old days to harden into persistent focus on the wrong things. Many leaders spend too much time staring into a rear-view mirror and forget that the images they see there are reversed, distorted, backward, and easily misinterpreted. The backward-facing mirrors on your car bear the warning, "objects in mirror are closer than they appear." In the same way, excessive attention to tradition, especially mindless replication of the wrong aspects of the past, will ensure that those old dangers sneak up on us and damage us again and again.

To put such obsession with staid tradition aside, examine the realities of the day, and act positively to support your convictions: This takes a courageous leader. It's what can make a Cubs' Fan leader and team a success.

8th Inning Discussion Questions

1. Is your organization too bound by tradition and the status quo? What can such an entity do to become more open to positive change?

2. Have you ever been part of an organization that had become satisfied with mediocrity? What might cause such a mindset? What could have made a difference for the better?

3. How does a leader's set of options and range of motivational tools differ depending upon whether the organization is for-profit, not-for-profit, governmental, religious, social, or another variation?

4. How can a leader motivate people who have long been retained and rewarded by an organizational culture that accepts mediocrity?

5. What one word would you choose to describe the way your organization handles underperforming employees?

6. Are poor performers within your team protected by powerful allies and/or systemic loopholes? If so, how has this happened? What initiatives might have a realistic prospect of correcting this?

7. How does the senior leadership in your organization view tradition? Do they have the equivalent of a no-night-baseball attitude with regard to any specific issue? How would you assess the balance they strike between revering past successes and making strategic changes to meet an evolving future?

8. Which of the following best captures your leadership philosophy: (1) If it ain't broke, don't fix it. (2) If it ain't broke, fix it anyway. (3) If it is broke, don't fix it.

9. How can a leader detect where wise perseverance ends and foolish refusal to face facts begins?

10. What are five advantages of leading an old, well-established organization? What are five advantages of leading a young, developing team?

11. What are some examples of leaders who refused to make adjustments long after there was clear evidence of failure?

9th INNING
100 Years Is Patience Run Amok

Patience may be a virtue, but complacency is a vice. It can be very helpful to maintain a long-term perspective, but equally harmful to harbor a passive, wait-till-some-year attitude. A vast chasm exists between obeying the law of the harvest (in which we carefully cultivate and work toward the eventual reward) and reaping what we sow through a defeatist culture, satisfied with whatever table scraps fall into our hands while we sit on our status quo. Success doesn't happen overnight, but if it hasn't come after 100 years it might possibly be time to shift a few paradigms.

We have identified nine innings worth of reasons why Cubs leadership has failed for a century to bring a World Championship trophy home to Wrigley Field. These flaws have sometimes acted alone, and sometimes in concert, to produce their sad outcome.

No fewer than 48 different managers have led the Cubs since they won their last title. That's right: 48 leaders, zero wins. By not detecting, let alone correcting, the underlying causes of defeat, the Dirty Four Dozen Cubs leaders have created the conditions for persistent tragedy. Any one of the errors discussed in the first eight innings of this book could justifiably be considered an Achilles' heel. That being said, the worst problem of all has become the neglectful refusal to search out and deal with the other problems. This is the most harmful Achilles' heel that has doomed the Cubs for 10 decades.

Here's the number one reason leaders fail, or fall short of their potential: An undiscovered and/or unhealed Achilles' heel—a weakness serious enough to negate all the many positive attributes the leaders may be blessed with. So here's one of the most important actions a leader can take: Find and rectify whatever hidden flaw threatens his or her future. This is unpleasant, painful, and arduous work, and thus why most people never do it. No off-the-shelf text on liposuction leadership can swiftly suck out our latent and long-festering vulnerability while we recline and rest. But unless we face our flaw, we gamble that one day our flaw will face us. In a moment, we can jeopardize everything we've achieved by a single unaddressed issue, and a career overflowing with attaboys is upended by one big oh-no.

Why are Achilles' heels so vulnerable, hard to detect, and difficult to correct? They're primarily caused by conflicts between two or more powerful and competing concerns. When this happens, a leader can be caught in the middle of a confusing and conflict-ridden dilemma. Let's illustrate with an example that draws from the main points of two or three of the earlier innings in this book.

We have discussed the dangers of prematurely assuming success, and the unrealistic overconfidence, arrogance, and carelessness that often accompany it. Consistent with this principle arises the need to be aware of potential risks, points of weakness within ourselves, and even possible disasters. Then we can train, prepare, practice, and take precautions that could help our team stay cool under pressure, less prone to panic.

But during our examination of the curse mentality and the devastatingly ill effects that come with a defeatist, pessimistic, and fatalist culture we also noted the importance of confidence, hope, optimism, positive incentives, and a forward-looking progressive mindset. An effective leader must accommodate all of these considerations in order to attain and maintain a healthy equilibrium. But how? The competing concerns at issue here are not necessarily mutually exclusive or contradictory; but they can be in tension. An overemphasis on one or more of them can create a serious Achilles' heel under some specific circumstances.

The leadership challenge is simple enough to state: We must simultaneously avoid, on the one hand, unwarranted overconfidence, brazen egomania, and a Pollyannaish assumption that everything is rosy; we must also steer clear, on the other hand, of gloomy pessimism, demoralizing preoccupation with failure, and a resigned hopelessness. In other words, the leader needs to balance optimism and pessimism, confidence and vulnerability, self-assurance and self-correction, learning from mistakes and moving beyond past errors, plus a relaxed sense of carefree fun and the concentrated determination to overcome adversity.

That's enough sets of opposites to fill a buffet tray of fortune cookies. What means are available to help a leader navigate this giant slalom of polar extremes? Think about your own experience trying to find and maintain the proper equilibrium as the context evolves, people come and go, the competition changes, personalities adjust, incentives shift, external pressures rise and fall, relationships grow and fracture, and myriad other variables modulate.

You know that the leader has to rely on some navigational aid to find his or her way through this obstacle course, complete with its ever-changing gauntlet of circumstances. But how? If you conceptualize this challenge as a mundane, real-world problem in moving safely and efficiently from one physical place to another, you might use several methods to assist you in finding your way. In no particular order of precision, they include: (1) Global Positioning System "G.P.S." device, (2) compass, (3) city street map, (4) state map, (5) national map, (6) a teammate playing "Marco Polo," (7) globe, (8) sextant, (9) aerial photographs, (10) a partner giving you "warmer" or "colder" clues, and (11) a Magic 8-Ball toy.

Personally, we might opt for the Magic 8-Ball if not for the fact that in our experience the only answer it ever gives is "NOT AT THIS TIME." But, come to think of it, that is usually the correct answer for whatever question we've asked; so maybe the Magic 8-Ball really does have some efficacy as a navigational aid.

Actually, the tools available to leaders are as imperfect, changeable, and imprecise as the challenges that face them. In the real world, a leader's task stands far more daunting than driving a car from one point to another (even in Boston), because of the pervasive influence of human factors, as well as constantly mutating pathways and obstacles. We might crave an easy panacea to neutralize this Achilles' heel—something along the lines of a user-friendly, inexpensive CD-ROM would be nice—but that is not the nature of this type of problem. No handy off-the-shelf software, flow chart, decision tree, go/no-go checklist, computerized BOT, artificial intelligence, or *Leadership for Lamebrains* primer will kiss it and make it all better for us.

We can begin to appreciate the magnitude of the challenge—and the reasons why a pattern of errors so often constitutes an Achilles' heel—when we frame the issue by considering a few ways our society has developed. With only a moderate amount of effort, we can compile a sizable list of clichés our culture has coined to synopsize the powerful forces on both sides of our dilemma. This many shopworn catch-phrases for and against these principles offer formidable, if circumstantial, evidence that these competing forces have existed for a very long time, exerting their considerable pull on a great many people. Let's list, in tabular form, some of the pairs of contestants in this age-old clash of the clichés.

SELF-CONFIDENCE	PANIC PREVENTION
What you don't know won't hurt you.	Knowledge is power.
Ignorance is bliss.	Forewarned is forearmed.
If you can conceive it and believe it, you can achieve it.	A little humble pie never hurt anybody.
Look on the bright side.	Get real.
Don't look back; something might be gaining on you.	Objects in a mirror are closer than they appear.
Accentuate the positive.	Eliminate the negative.
Don't worry, be happy.	Save for a rainy day.
Look at the glass as half full, not half empty.	Prepare for the worst.
Damn the torpedoes, full speed ahead!	Slow down, dangerous curves ahead.
Don't stop thinking about tomorrow.	Those who refuse to learn from the past are doomed to repeat it.
Don't sweat the small stuff, and it's all small stuff.	The devil is in the details.
Don't prepare to fight the last war.	Past is prologue.
If you can dream it, you can do it.	Wake up and smell the coffee.
What, me worry?	Look before you leap.
Fortune favors the bold.	Better safe than sorry.
We have nothing to fear but fear itself.	Anything that can go wrong, will go wrong.

Without a leadership vision acutely attuned to all of these complexities and subtleties, our individual biases and preferences will supply the added throw-weight. That will tip the balance in favor of one set of assumptions, for better or worse. Avoidance of this trap takes a sophisticated, finely-tuned appreciation of perspective and balance, a judicious tipping-point equilibration.

In the above list of competing concerns, the negative Mr. Hyde facets of both poles are the Scylla and Charybdis between which a Cubs Fan leader must navigate. There is no generic, one-size-fits-all model approach... and to assume there is amounts to a dangerous Achilles' heel. Rather, the optimal plan would be a flexible, evolving, living matrix that is sensitive to context, personalities, team experience, collective strengths, and internal challenges. We can list and assign relative weights to relevant factors and variables, and maybe construct a working model of interrelationships among them; but we will never succeed in creating a formulaic, machine-like panacea.

Some leaders succumb to a built-in bias, favoring one set of considerations over the other. Depending on how this tips the scales, we might view the very same situation as healthy self-esteem or delusional over-confidence; fearless swagger or cocky presumptuousness; relaxed assurance or cavalier arrogance; and positive expectation of success or unrealistic insouciance.

Similarly, depending on the lens we're peering through, we could see either pragmatic acknowledgement of risks or undue pessimism; prudent disaster readiness or unbalanced overemphasis or worst-case contingencies; sound historical perspective or tension-laden preoccupation with past failures; disciplined self-assessment or obsession with negativity; and constant quality improvement or burdensome dwelling on remote dangers. No litmus paper or cookbook recipe has ever been invented that can properly make these exquisitely nuanced, multi-layered, context-sensitive judgments for us. It is precisely because these and other challenges are so non-linear and infinitely varied that recurring errors in judgment constitute an Achilles' heel that can bring down any leader.

Earlier in this book we reviewed some lessons gleaned from the Cubs' 1969 roller coaster season. As we end the book with a discussion of leadership Achilles' heels, we will consider one more example from 1969. Naturally, it will be a bad example.

The Cubs' leader that year was veteran manager Leo Durocher. Durocher had been in baseball for decades, and had even played alongside Babe Ruth. He had a well-earned reputation as a very strict, extremely demanding manager. His players knew that he expected them to push themselves, and even to play when injured, for the greater good of the entire team. Durocher never settled for less than full effort at all times from his players, and he wasn't above criticizing them in the press if he felt they weren't giving the team all they had. Unfortunately, Leo had an Achilles' heel in terms of his own priorities, and it caused him and the Cubs tremendous harm.

In late July, the Cubs were riding high atop their division. The Achilles' heel began to flare up on July 26, Durocher's 63rd birthday. In the middle of a game against the Los Angeles Dodgers, Durocher told one of his coaches that he felt sick and was going to leave. In Durocher's absence, the coach took over the leadership duties for the remainder of the game, and for the next game as well. The team doctor made an announcement the following day that Leo was confined to his quarters, suffering from "gastritis." But then it came to light that Durocher was not ill at all. Instead, he had secretly left his team mid-game to travel to Eagle River in northern Wisconsin, where he participated in "Parents' Weekend" at Camp Ojibwa. While the Cubs were playing baseball for the pennant, Leo attended an outing at the summer camp where his new wife's 12-year-old son was enjoying his vacation. He returned to Chicago a day later and rejoined the team, having missed one full game and most of another.

Quite a media furor erupted once the news came in from Camp Ojibwa. One Chicago reporter described it as "calling in sick and playing hooky from a baseball game." Reports ensued of a highly contentious meeting between Durocher and team owner Philip K. Wrigley, and even intimations that Wrigley had fired Durocher. However, the owner and the manager somehow worked out a mutual understanding, and the Cubs headed into August with Leo Durocher still at the helm. The prodigal manager didn't apologize to his team, and went back to work essentially trying to pretend the whole thing had never happened. But everyone on the Cubs knew better.

It is impossible to gauge exactly what impact the Camp Ojibwa incident had on the Cubs team. In conjunction with other events, it couldn't have helped. Veteran, aging players wilted in the late summer heat, weary from playing so many day games in the glaring sunshine of light-free Wrigley Field. Durocher's tendency to overwork his older stars, and his demands that they play through injuries, became more aggravating in the aftermath of his personal malingering, deceit, and selfishness. Team morale and unity already had been badly shaken before this controversy (because of the Don Young fiasco), and Durocher's evident hypocrisy could only have intensified the damage. Within the broader context of the Don Young incident and the eventual black cat debacle, this proved the worst kind of Achilles' heel for the Cubs' manager, under the circumstances.

The Camp Ojibwa dust-up happened 37 years before the ground-breaking Disney Channel Original Movie *High School Musical* made the song "We're All In This Together" the anthem for another generation. When the phenomenally successful 2007 sequel *High School Musical 2* added another hymn to unity, "All For One," it came nearly four decades too late to save Durocher and the Cubs from themselves. But the lessons from those great songs aren't new. Leaders have always known the central importance of personally embodying the same qualities they expect from their teams. Leaders who demand as much or more from themselves as they do from their followers reap the harvest of increased unity and enhanced collective strength. Leaders who do the opposite only succeed in serving up themselves and their teams as fodder for what-went-wrong books for generations to come.

What went through the minds of dedicated Cubs veterans like Ernie Banks, Don Kessinger, Glenn Beckert, and Randy Hundley during the dog days of the pennant race when Durocher asked them to continue playing every day despite oppressive heat and humidity, nagging injuries, and debilitating fatigue? What did workhorse pitchers like Fergie Jenkins think when Durocher criticized them as selfish quitters? How did ironman Billy Williams feel, playing every single game year after year, when his manager lied to the team and went to summer camp in the middle of a pennant race? What emotions did rookie Don Young experience when the leader, who just weeks earlier had ripped him for making costly mistakes, made one of his own and thought no apologies were necessary? When the Cubs' once-huge lead in the standings evaporated and the team had to fight the "Miracle Mets" for the pennant in August and September, the contrast between Durocher's standards for his players and what he tolerated in himself must have created a cancer in their morale, cohesiveness, and spirit.

At a time when the Cubs most desperately needed an inspirational leader they could trust, respect, and emulate, they found only a hypocritical, self-serving, work-shirking, illness-faking liar. That critical vulnerability—that Achilles' heel—brought down the Cubs as surely as if they had been pierced by a fatal arrow.

The metaphor of Achilles' heel is a potent one, because legendary Achilles himself stood as a demigod and the greatest warrior who ever lived, virtually a one-man army capable of winning battles for whatever side he favored with his unmatched abilities. He could slay the enemies' premier hero, even Hector of Troy, and conquer the mightiest of obstacles. Yet his famous heel was ever present throughout his astonishing string of marvelous triumphs; and at the climax of his crowning victory over Troy it allowed him to be killed by a far inferior enemy. If a lowly heel could fell the ultimate military genius at the pinnacle of his power, every leader would do well to check carefully for whatever vulnerability threatens his or her own success.

That doesn't mark such self-inspection as fun or easy. No one, from Achilles on down, likes to confront his or her own imperfections—especially faults deep and deadly enough to provoke utter failure. Sometimes we actually remain unaware of our own worst weaknesses, at least on a conscious level, simply because we find it far more comfortable to avoid them, pretending all is fine. We won't wrestle with such pernicious internal perils.

Moreover, some character defects only manifest themselves when a particular, specific combination of unusual circumstances coalesces, which might not happen more than once or twice in a lifetime, if at all. It can be challenging and repugnant work to stare long and closely at ourselves in a starkly-lit mirror, trying to identify those often well-concealed weaknesses. It involves methodical analysis of often horrible memories: incidents in which things went very wrong. It forces us to ask ourselves when and why this happened, has this recurred, or could it recur?

It is infinitely easier, and far more enjoyable, to spot Achilles' heels in other leaders than to turn the harsh searchlight on ourselves. At least since Biblical times people have exhibited a strong preference for seeing the speck in others' eyes while looking past the two-by-four in their own. If we indulge in this venerable spectator's sport, it doesn't take long to compile a reasonably formidable list of some of the most common, and most dangerous, character flaws that have plagued and even ruined famous leaders throughout history (though certainly not ourselves). Perhaps you could add to the following partial roster of Achilles' heels:

1. Greed/selfishness
2. Dishonesty
3. Egomania
4. Addiction to drugs, alcohol, sex, or gambling/risk
5. Bias/prejudice
6. Unfairness/tendency to play favorites
7. Lack of courage
8. Inability to accept criticism
9. Untrustworthiness
10. Sense of special entitlement/exemption from rules and laws
11. Uncontrolled temper
12. Feeling of infallibility/invincibility
13. Insecurity
14. Disloyalty
15. Recklessness/acute impatience
16. Lack of foresight/inability to plan
17. Disdain for others/absence of empathy
18. Obsession with/fanaticism for an ideology
19. Overwhelming ambition
20. Unwillingness to receive bad news
21. Cruelty
22. Grandiose belief in one's own destiny for greatness
23. Excessive indecision/immersion in trivial details
24. Refusal to learn pertinent facts before making decisions
25. Insistence on blind obedience and sycophancy
26. Tendency to panic in crises
27. Closed-mindedness
28. Paranoia

29. Inability to trust others
30. Gullibility
31. Hypersensitivity
32. Need to control everything personally
33. Carelessness/penchant to lose focus or concentration on key details
34. Excessive obstinacy
35. Refusal to accept blame/responsibility
36. Procrastination
37. Rigidity/inflexibility or resistance to positive change
38. Emotional inaccessibility/incapacity to relate to others
39. Intolerance of any imperfection in products or people
40. Vindictiveness/vengefulness and unwillingness to forgive
41. Incapacity to "read" others/deal with people normally
42. Obliviousness to the impression/effect one has on others
43. Jealousy/envy
44. Hypocrisy
45. Unreliability in honoring promises and obligations
46. Refusal to delegate
47. All-consuming hatred or anger
48. Immaturity
49. Hyper-emotionalism
50. Loner mindset/inability to be a team player

Some of these prominent character weaknesses tend to be linked, and to overlap and combine with others. They may be symptomatic of more fundamental traits that have multiple manifestations; conversely, some traits may be inconsistent with others and unlikely to co-exist in the same individual. Unfortunately, any given person may have several Achilles' heels, even if limited by Nature to only two actual foot-rooted heels. This applies even to relatively independent traits, so that a person might be greedy, have an uncontrolled temper, and lack courage as well (in a veritable trifecta of defects).

Here you see one of the remarkable aspects of the human race: Our capacity to prove our imperfection, beyond the shadow of a doubt, and to prove it in multiple ways. Indeed, we could supplement this distasteful list indefinitely, with as many variations on the major themes as in a mammoth, human-filled game of Sudoku.

All of us could effortlessly critique many leaders, great and not-so-great, ancient and modern, and catalogue the flaw or cluster of flaws that undermined them. From Julius Caesar, Hannibal, and Alexander the Great to Ronald Reagan, Bill Clinton, and George W. Bush (not to mention Leo Durocher), it is so easy for us to play Name That Heel. One wonders why these exceptionally powerful individuals didn't do it themselves, and proactively root out all those inimical defects. How could they not see their glaring blind spots? Why would such successful and eminently experienced leaders make colossal blunders, and even make them repeatedly, when the consequences seem so obvious and predictable to us in our retrospection recliners? We can help ourselves to a few cheap laughs at the Big Boys' expense. But then, when it is our turn to literally help ourselves by putting our own character under the microscope, the game jumps suddenly to a much more challenging and decidedly less festive level.

If we refuse to search for and deal with our own Achilles' heel, though, we are rolling the dice with our entire careers on the line. We are betting that we will be lucky enough never to have the peculiar concatenation of opportunity, stimuli, timing, and situation mesh together in our lives, causing our most critical vulnerability to be fatally pierced. We might get away with it. We might run out of life before we run out of luck. Or maybe our exploited weakness will be rescued by other, more favorable circumstances and all will not be lost. But that's a lot of gambling for a good leader on whom so many people are depending. Introspection—intense self-examination, with all possible honesty—can allow us to gain crucial awareness of that which could destroy us. With that awareness can come a plan to overcome it, or at least contain the damage.

It may not be possible to completely eliminate our greatest weakness, given that it likely was forged through many years of experience; the Cubs have thoroughly illustrated that point. But at a minimum we ought to be able to identify and then stay away from those specific temptations, situations, preconditions, and circumstances that have proved their potential to breach weakness and thereby cause our downfall. By gaining cognizance of the existence and nature of our Achilles' heel, we acquire the opportunity to become alert to whatever warning signals tip off the approach of our special combination of dangerous conditions, and therefore to exercise extra caution to guard against giving in to our weakness.

Oscar Wilde famously yet erroneously declared, "The only way to get rid of a temptation is to yield to it." But actually the best remedy is to understand the temptation and what causes it, strive constantly to remain removed from those causes, stay vigilant for early signs of trouble, and then use all our strength to resist surrender. Doing nothing along these lines makes it far more probable that, one day, people will be gossiping about our own stunning failure, shaking their heads that we could throw our once-promising career away on something so blatantly foolish, so entirely obvious (to others) that we should never have been caught up in it. Finding and healing our Achilles' heel (or heels) can be one of the greatest favors we ever do for ourselves, our people, and our organization. For this to happen, leaders must work hard at building character, making a difference, and changing lives.

Baseball fans everywhere will long remember the most famous Achilles' heel, literally speaking, in sports history. Boston Red Sox starting pitcher Curt Schilling turned in one of the most courageous sports performances ever when he pitched his team to a key win over the Yankees in Game Six of the 2004 American League Championship Series. Despite suffering a serious injury to his right ankle earlier in the series, Schilling took the mound and bravely went after the Yankee batters. There was no margin for error, no room for defeat. If the Red Sox had lost, they would have been eliminated and sent home for the winter, so Schilling knew he would have to get past his pain for the sake of his team.

Blood from a ruptured tendon sheath seeped visibly through Schilling's sock like a red badge of courage during the game, but he pressed on, and won. His heel bled badly again in Game Two of the World Series, but that didn't stop Schilling either. He won again. That's what leaders must do. We all have some Achilles' heel. What makes all the difference is what we do about it. Schilling overcame his obstacle, and one of his famous bloody socks is now enshrined in the Hall of Fame. But all too often the Cubs have succumbed to theirs.

It is a sad but revealing commentary on our jaded, skeptical times that some even doubted the legitimacy of Schilling's famous bloody sock. In 2007, some critics publicly suggested that it was paint, not blood, on

Schilling's sock during his playoff victory against the Yankees, and that it was done as a publicity stunt. Schilling was understandably outraged by this accusation, and offered to bet $1 million on the matter. There were no takers. But the whole incident illustrates how difficult it is for some people to believe that anyone can become a genuine hero. No matter how powerful the evidence, some of us are so inured to scandal and hypocrisy that we see an Achilles' heel everywhere we look, even in the blood-soaked heel of a true champion. It is this virulent strain of heartsick disenchantment that every leader today must confront, and overcome.

The Chicago Cubs exemplify all of the Achilles' heels and corresponding curative principles discussed in this book, for better or for worse. Some of these same characteristics exist in many other organizations in fields of endeavor far different from professional sports, and their effects have a profound influence on success or failure. It can be instructive to analyze the Cubs as a famous example of missed opportunities, mismatched incentives, and entrenched negativity.

The Cubs' triple-digit World Championship drought is appalling in its own right. For any professional team to break through the double-digit barrier is a remarkable feat of sustained futility by any yardstick. There's something inherently awe-inspiring about numbers of 100 or more, an intangible power that lower figures can't match in psychological throw-weight. It would be great if the Cubs' hundreds-hubbub had been in the positive category, of course, but you take your records where you earn them when you're the Cubs.

There is a context within which the Cubs' century of senselessness becomes even more striking. As the accompanying chart illustrates, a stampede of freshly-minted expansion teams have made it to the World Series, and even won the title during the Cubs' 100-year championship famine that began in 1909. In fact, all of this dizzying expansion-team success has taken place much more recently than the last time the Cubs were in the World Series at all—the Harry-Truman year 1945. There were never any expansion teams whatsoever in baseball until 1961; but that didn't stop several of them from leaving the Cubs—charter members of the National League since its inception in 1876—in their dust, or in their champagne bubbles. Adding insult to ignominy, two of the very youngest expansion franchises have already notched not one but two World Championships during their exceedingly brief history.

Expansion Team	Year Team Began	Year in World Series
L.A./Anaheim Angels	1961	2002
New York Mets	1962	1969, 1986 (lost in 2000)
Houston Astros	1962	(lost in 2005)
San Diego Padres	1969	(lost in 1984, 1998)
Kansas City Royals	1969	1985
Seattle Pilots/Mil. Brewers	1969	(Brewers lost in 1983)
Toronto Blue Jays	1977	1992, 1993
Colorado Rockies	1993	(lost in 2007)
Florida Marlins	1993	1997, 2003
Ariz. Diamondbacks	1998	2001
Tampa Bay (Devil) Rays	1998	(lost in 2008)

The Blue Jays took only 15 years from their 1977 inception to win their first World Series in 1992. Then they promptly did an encore performance the next year—two World Championships by the time the team was 16 years young. But as spectacular as Toronto's achievement was, the Marlins topped it. They literally dashed from zeroes to heroes. A mere four years after their 1993 creation, the Marlins became champions in 1997...and then they did it again on their 10th birthday in 2003. Of course their 2003 title came partially through the courtesy of the Cubs' post-Bartman meltdown, but it still adds up to two World Series crowns during the first 10 years of the Marlins' existence. *Ten years* and *two* world titles? The Cubs have gone *10 decades* with *zero* World Championships!

During the entire expansion-team era since 1961, no fewer than six of the new teams have already captured one or more World Series. Five more expansion franchises have made it to the World Series but without yet taking home the big prize. Since the very first World Series was played in 1903, the only teams without even one trip to the Fall Classic are three expansion teams (Montreal Expos/Washington Nationals, Seattle Mariners, and the "new" Washington Senators/Texas Rangers), none of which was created before 1969. Therefore, a total of 11 of the new franchises have already reached the Series, as against three that have not...all since 1961. Compared to the Cubs' ancient/most recent World Series Championship in 1908 and their latest (pre-Cold War) ticket to the Series in 1945, this slew of nouveau-riche upstart triumphs happened in a New York nanosecond.

A Cubs Fan leader contemplates this situation and asks a few questions. How can brand-new organizations race from team birth to Series berth in as little as four years? Isn't there any competitive advantage that accompanies being in continuous operation since 1876? How can completely new teams swiftly assemble a championship winner when they start out with nothing but other teams' rejects and raw rookies? What, if any, edge comes from not having a long history? If some older teams (like the Cardinals, in the National League since 1892 and winners of 10 World Series) seem to use their lengthy existence as a firm foundation, why do the Cubs perform as if theirs were a coffin lid? Are there lessons old-time organizations sometimes can learn from comparative youngsters?

We've shown how the Cubs' longevity comes with weighty, awkward baggage well beyond most teams' carry-on limit. Constant reminders of past failures, coupled with intense pressure from fans and aggressive news media to break ancient mythical curses, have shackled Cubs players and managers with a burden that couldn't possibly be present for a new organization. Also, there is the danger that prior mistakes will be replicated when they spring from old, deeply ingrained, bad habits. Poor structures, processes, policies, and incentive systems—if left in place for many years—can come to cling tenaciously around an organization's vulnerable neck like a Velcro albatross.

A young, fresh organization experiences much less risk of being imprisoned by the shackles of the way things have always been done, simply because "always" means nothing more than "recently" to the new group. If the leader of a relatively new team proactively avoids the Achilles' heels we've listed in this inning, he or she usually has much greater freedom to innovate, experiment, and build the unit in whatever manner best fits the circumstances. That puts the leader ahead of the head of an antiquated organization where the people and the system are more rigid and less open to new approaches. Maybe most important of all, a lively young crowd can produce abundant positive energy and find enjoyment—and even joy—in every challenge, while battle-scarred veterans see only tension, ghosts of old failures, and risk of further collapse. The rookies often have fun and relax while the veterans, who know first-hand how deeply it hurts to lose, become so tense and worried that they forget how to breathe. The difference in outcomes is every bit as dramatic as the difference in outlooks, and is almost entirely attributable to that attitude gap. A spectator can often see the difference written on the players' faces—smiles and laughter for the novices, furrowed brows and grim frowns for the old-timers. Bewildered veterans frequently shake their heads at this phenomenon as they wonder aloud whether the over-achieving youngsters don't know enough to be scared...and maybe silently wishing that they too could be that comfortable under pressure.

Let's consider the phenomenon of expansion-team success in terms of the Coefficient of Panic Vulnerability (C.P.V.) we introduced in the 4th Inning. It may be counterintuitive, but many expansion teams may have a lower (more favorable) C.P.V. than veteran, far more experienced clubs. Inherent in a new organization's freshness is a relative lack of any experience from prior crises, whether positive or negative. This experience dearth limits a young team's ability to capitalize on lessons derived from prior trials, but it also frees the group from the crushing negative effects of former failures under pressure. Without a record of demoralizing failures hanging around their necks, team members find no reason to shout, "Oh, no! Here we go again!" This overreaction to the first sign of adversity has plagued the Cubs so many times, even after such brilliant regular-season successes as in 2008. In other words, when an emergency situation threatens to get out of hand, it is better to have no experiences in earlier crises rather than bad ones. This is apparent from an examination of a new team's typical values for the variables that comprise C.P.V.

Usually a recently formed organization with mostly young members will have little or no collective or individual experience with prior emergencies, either of the positive or negative variety. Thus, both E_n and E_p will be very small with the difference between them negligible, and this tends to reduce the overall C.P.V. Also, the S variable will be low because it is quite unlikely that any exigent circumstances will prove similar to something the team faced before, and this too will bring the C.P.V. down.

Furthermore, the perceived risk (R) may often be minuscule, simply because all the novices don't know enough to be worried. Young, inexperienced professionals tend to be untainted by past injuries and collapses, and are blessed with an abundance of youthful confidence, fun-affinity, and sense of invulnerability or immortality. Even when not objectively justified, this attitude can help insulate a team of rookies from the tension-laden pressure that causes older veteran units to fold like a house of cards. The combination of all these minimum-value factors in the C.P.V. numerator pulls an expansion team's vulnerability to panic way down.

There is also good news in this for whoever is leading an inexperienced organization. Given that such an inchoate team will often have a small numerator in its C.P.V., a great opportunity exists for a leader to bring the overall C.P.V. down even more by working on the factors most within the leader's control. A leader can exert beneficial influence on the T and L factors in the C.P.V. denominator by selectively concentrating on realistic and effective panic-prevention training, and by refining his or her own leadership skills.

If the leader succeeds in either or both of these efforts, the denominator will increase and the overall C.P.V. will shrink. It is not uncommon for an expansion-type team to have the highly favorable profile in which the C.P.V. numerator is small, the denominator large, and the total vulnerability to panic extremely low. Again, this combination of factors tends to make a new, youthful team much more resilient, relaxed, unafraid, and resistant to panic under intense pressure than many groups of battle-hardened—and all too often battle-scarred/shell-shocked—veterans.

The leader of a new organization largely staffed with eager young people will often find C.P.V. management easier than with a more mature, experience-laden unit. There is very little need to undo past mistakes, or to unlearn bad lessons. Plus, the natural energy and verve of the rookies will help the organization acquire some success stories, unburdened by the need to cope with prior disasters. The leader who wants to write a positive message will find a blank page so much more ready than a crumpled old one filled with unhelpful messages that need to be erased before anything new can be written. All the energy and determination required to painstakingly rub out that negative scribbling on an old sheet of paper can be devoted instead to crafting a positive statement from the outset. When a panic-sparking crisis erupts, good experience is better than bad (or none), but no experience at all is also preferable to a ton of rusty old baggage. At least you begin the race fresh and unfettered from a clean, level starting line and not from the bottom of a deep, dark, greasy pit with a bulky backpack on your shoulders.

These are just some of the reasons why so many novice expansion teams have out-performed the iconic Chicago Cubs. The leader of a venerable, mature organization like the Cubs must realize this: Not all traditions are worth keeping, and unsuccessful results deserve a hard look to see whether there's a better approach available. A leader who sets the tone and exemplifies the right attitude can make a huge difference for an older organization, but only if he or she is determined to remain open to good ideas from whatever source, and to restore a sense of fun and excitement wherever possible. That's how expansion teams beat charter members of the league, again and again. Excessive patience, in the form of stubborn opposition to change, is one of a leader's worst Achilles' heels. It can permanently trap an organization in an infinite cycle of futility where there is no champagne, only pain.

For most of us (thankfully) our leadership blunders are not on public display for millions of intensely interested people to second-guess. We can all benefit, though, from the very conspicuous failures of the Cubs, and incorporate the vicarious lessons learned into our own repertoire of ideas. In truth, leadership has many commonalities irrespective of the level of public scrutiny, and regardless of whether the field of activity is Wrigley Field, private business, or government service. When we analyze the mistakes and lost opportunities of others, and adjust our approach accordingly, we can save ourselves and our team the heartache that awaits those who do not.

The Cubs are now beginning their second hundred years without a World Championship to show for all their exertions. By virtue of sheer random chance they should have been able to win a title more recently than the Roosevelt Administration (Teddy, not Franklin). In our own lives and careers, we can't count on anyone steadfastly sticking with us through a couple of bad years, let alone a century or more of failure. Whether we go to work every day in the Ivy League or the ivy-walled Wrigley Field, patience has its limits. When hopelessness springs eternal, it's time to figure out why. That's why we wrote this book. Every leader can take some lessons from the Cubs' thick catalogue of catastrophes, and then take action to steer toward better results. This year may not be "Next Year" for the Cubs, but it can be for the rest of us.

Finally, for our readers who, like us, remain lifelong Cubs fans, allow us to conclude this book on a personal note. Those who pin their dreams on the Cubs' fortunes inevitably are enriched by the many highs and lows the Cubs conjure up on their wild, enduring quest for Neverland. Followers of most other teams cannot begin to understand what it is like to love a team, deeply and faithfully, through a whole century without even one World Championship.

When titles come often, easily, and without long droughts, people can begin to take them for granted, to expect them every year, and even to demand them as a precondition to their continued support. But the Cubs don't attract fair-weather fans, for reasons that should be entirely obvious. People don't become, or remain, Cubs fans if they want to back a perennial winner and capture World Series bragging rights at least a few times every decade. Front-runners want to lend (not give, lend) their support to what they think is a sure thing, or close to it. They are not interested in cheering for a team that fails to make the postseason, let alone loses more games than it wins. They want to be winners automatically, by default. They aren't Cubs fans.

A true fan, like a true friend, sticks around even when it isn't fun, and even when it hurts. When someone stays loyal when it isn't popular, or easy, or cool, the motivations must run much deeper than a superficial taste for acceptance and acclaim.

Cubs fans know what it feels like to have their hearts crushed, again and again, and yet to keep on loving. Cubs fans learn early what it takes to remain faithful to what they believe in, no matter what tragedies and bitter disappointments befall them. Cubs fans live the truth that we can never control everything life might throw at us, but we can always control our own reactions. Cubs fans grasp how to hold on tightly to beautiful dreams, even when many of them end up as nightmares. Cubs fans spend their lives waiting for a wish to come true, staying around for lifetimes worth of faith, enduring through prolonged seasons of sadness for that fairytale ending so long postponed.

That breed of steadfastness sometimes seems like an anachronism in the post-modern age, as old-fashioned and outmoded a vintage as Wrigley Field's verdant vine-yard itself. But being a Cubs fan isn't effortless, and neither is life. People who devotedly stand by the Cubs through all the losses, curses, endless waiting, collapses, incompetence, near-misses, and broken promises are different in the best possible sense of the word. They don't blow away when a stiff, icy breeze swoops hard off Lake Michigan. Their fealty doesn't evaporate when the fun times stop. Their fidelity isn't transferable to the latest fashionable fad. Their love doesn't skip away when you need it most. They are strong, dependable, enduring, rugged survivors. They are the people we all want as our friends. And they are the people we all need as our leaders.

9th Inning Discussion Questions

1. What Achilles' heels can you identify in contemporary prominent leaders?

2. How have famous leaders throughout history dealt with, or failed to deal with, their Achilles' heels? What have been the consequences?

3. Consider the "clash of clichés" table in light of a major leadership challenge you've recently faced. How have you attempted to achieve a healthy balance between the principles underlying the optimistic self-confidence and realistic panic-prevention ideas? Did you overemphasize one set of concerns to the detriment of your overall effectiveness?

4. What are your own Achilles' heels? How have they affected your life and your career?

5. Is there anyone in your life who knows you well enough to have a valid opinion as to your most vulnerable Achilles' heel? If so, take a deep breath and ask them for their honest opinion on this issue. What is the one thing you hope they would not tell you?

6. What are three things you can begin to work on today to lessen your vulnerability to your Achilles' heels?

7. How can you identify Achilles' heels in your organization and in your workers? How can you assist your workers in finding and making adjustments for their Achilles' heels?

8. How do you, as a leader, evaluate each of the following errors in terms of seriousness and your determination to avoid them? (a) Giving up on a worthy course of action too early due to over-cautiousness and fear. (b) Staying the course too long on a doomed enterprise due to ignoring warning signals and excessive obstinacy. (c) Folding a sound policy because of unwillingness to withstand criticism from those inside and outside your organization.

9. If a squad of investigative reporters had been embedded within your organization for the past year, what headline would they write to summarize their report on your leadership style? What would be their three main findings?

10. Some think that leadership is a lot like surgery: it is traumatic, tedious, and emotionally draining. Do you believe this is true? How could you make the negative factors work in your favor?

11. What are some advantages and disadvantages of a young, inexperienced group of people versus an older, more stress-tested group? How can a leader best help both types of organizations?

12. Do you think a relatively new organization with many novices necessarily has a better C.P.V. than older, more experienced units? What else would you want to know about the young team before you could confidently predict its vulnerability to panic under the stress of an emergency?

Bibliography and Recommended Reading

Adair, Robert K. *The Physics of Baseball*. New York, HarperCollins, 2002.

Block, David. *Baseball Before We Knew It: A Search for the Roots of the Game.* Lincoln, University of Nebraska Press, 2005.

Creamer, Robert W. *Babe: The Legend Comes to Life.* New York, Simon and Shuster, 1974.

Dawidoff, Nicholas. *Baseball: A Literary Anthology.* New York, Library of America: Distributed to the trade in the U.S. by Penguin, 2002.

Feldman, Doug and Don Kessinger. *Miracle Collapse: The 1969 Chicago Cubs.* Lincoln, University of Nebraska Press, 2006.

Fleder, Rob. **The Baseball Book.** New York, Sports Illustrated Books/Time Inc. Home Entertainment, 2006.

Golenbock, Peter. *Wrigleyville: A Magical History Tour of the Chicago Cubs.* New York, St. Martin's Press, 1996.

Honig, Donald. *Baseball America: The Heroes of the Game and the Times of Their Glory.* New York, Macmillan, 1985.

Johnson, Steve. *The Chicago Cubs Yesterday & Today.* Voyageur Press, 2008.

Kahn, Roger. *Memories of Summer: When Baseball was an Art and Writing About It a Game.* New York, Hyperion, 1997.

Lechner, Tammy and Billy Williams. **The Chicago Cubs: Our Team, Our Dream: A Cub's Fan's Journey into Baseball's Greatest Romance.** Triumph Books, 2007.

Montville, Leigh. *The Big Bam: The Life and Times of Babe Ruth.* New York, Doubleday, 2006.

Reisler, Jim. *Babe Ruth: Launching the Legend.* New York, McGraw-Hill, 2004.

Ross, Alan. *Cubs Pride: For the Love of Ernie, Fergie & Wrigley.* Cumberland House, 2005.

Stout, Glenn and Richard A. Johnson. *The Cubs: The Complete Story of Chicago Cubs Baseball.* Houghton Mifflin, 2007.

Tygiel, Jules. *Past Time: Baseball as History.* Oxford [England]; New York, Oxford University Press, 2000.

Vecsey, George. *Baseball: A History of America's Favorite Game.* New York, Modern Library, 2006.

Vorwald, Bob and Steven Green. *Cubs Forever: Memories from the Men Who Lived Them.* Triumph Books, 2008.

Walken, Peter. *99 and Counting: Life as a Chicago Cubs Fan.* BookSurge Publishing, 2008.

Ward, Geoffrey C. *Baseball: An Illustrated History.* New York, A.A. Knopf, Distributed by Random House, 1994.

Will, George F. *Men at Work: The Craft of Baseball.* New York, Macmillan, 1990.

Index